WORLD WAR 1 FOR TEENS

AMAZING FACTS, KEY PLAYERS, HEROIC ACTS, MAJOR BATTLES, AND HOW THE WAR CHANGED THE WORLD

JAMES BURROWS

© Copyright 2023 - All rights reserved.

The content contained within this book may not be reproduced, duplicated or transmitted without direct written permission from the author or the publisher.

Under no circumstances will any blame or legal responsibility be held against the publisher, or author, for any damages, reparation, or monetary loss due to the information contained within this book, either directly or indirectly.

Legal Notice:

This book is copyright protected. It is only for personal use. You cannot amend, distribute, sell, use, quote or paraphrase any part, or the content within this book, without the consent of the author or publisher.

Disclaimer Notice:

Please note the information contained within this document is for educational and entertainment purposes only. All effort has been executed to present accurate, up to date, reliable, complete information. No warranties of any kind are declared or implied. Readers acknowledge that the author is not engaged in the rendering of legal, financial, medical or professional advice. The content within this book has been derived from various sources. Please consult a licensed professional before attempting any techniques outlined in this book.

By reading this document, the reader agrees that under no circumstances is the author responsible for any losses, direct or indirect, that are incurred as a result of the use of the information contained within this document, including, but not limited to, errors, omissions, or inaccuracies.

CONTENTS

Introduction	ix
1. WHAT CAUSED WORLD WAR 1?	1
The Concert of Europe Falls Apart	2
The Balkan Powder Keg	3
The Assassination of the Archduke	4
War Declarations	5
2. WHICH COUNTRIES TOOK PART IN THE WAR?	7
Central Powers	8
Allied Powers	9
3. LEADERS AND GENERALS	13
Allied Political Leaders and Military Generals	14
Central Powers Political Leaders and Military Generals	22
4. WORLD WAR 1 IN NUMBERS	27
Outrageous Numbers	27
Startling Amounts	29
Deadly Figures	31
5. TACTICS AND TECHNOLOGY	35
Changing Tactics	35
New Technologies	40
6. TIMELINE OF THE WAR	49
1914	49
1915	52
1916	53
1917	54
1918	56
1919	58
7. MAJOR EVENTS & BATTLES - 1914	59
Siege of Liege	60
Germany Loses Colonies	61
Serbian Campaign	62

Battle of the Frontiers	63
Battle of Tannenberg	64
First Battle of the Marne	66
First Battle of Ypres	67
Christmas Truce	69
8. MAJOR EVENTS & BATTLES - 1915	71
Gallipoli	71
Second Battle of Ypres	73
Gorlice-Tarnow Offensive	75
Battle of Loos	76
Siege of Kut	78
9. MAJOR EVENTS & BATTLES - 1916	81
Battle of Verdun	81
Battle of Jutland	83
Brusilov Offensive	85
Battle of the Somme	86
10. MAJOR EVENTS & BATTLES - 1917	89
Vimy Ridge	89
Messines	91
Third Battle of Ypres	92
Battle of Cambrai	93
11. MAJOR EVENTS & BATTLES - 1918 AND HOW THE WAR ENDED	95
Spring Offensive	95
Battle of Amiens	98
Battle of Megiddo	99
Meuse-Argonne Offensive	101
12. LIFE IN THE TRENCHES	103
Mud	103
Stink	104
Pests	105
Rations	106
Routine	107
Shell Shock	109
13. HEROIC FEATS	111
Military	112
Medical	121

Communications	123
Spies	125
14. HOW THE WAR CHANGED THE WORLD	129
Geo-Political	130
False Peace	132
Social	134
Epidemic	135
Technology	136
Financial	137
Memorials	139
Conclusions	143
About the Author	147
References	149

Dedicated to my great-grandfather, Robert Charles Caston, who fought at the Somme, and to all those that have fought for our freedoms.

INTRODUCTION

Wars had been fought for centuries, but never one like this! This was the Great War.

Kings, emperors, and sultans threw armies at each other for the sake of ruling—the blood of battle was an age-old tradition to protect what was yours or try to take what wasn't yours, while the rest looked on. Neighbors never got involved in another country's disputes if they could help it.

World War 1 was different. For the first time in history, almost everybody that was anybody at that time jumped into the quarrel. Nations were taking sides against other nations, backing their allies, knowing that the outcome would change the face of Europe and how wars would be fought in the future. The Central Powers (Germany, Austria-Hungary, and Turkey) opposed the Allies (France, Great Britain, Russia, Italy, Japan, and later, the United States).

It was supposed to be the one that would stop all the fighting once and for all—a war that would end all wars.

20 million people lost their lives over the course of five years; more deaths than in any of the battles fought before it. It would be

INTRODUCTION

the first time that a war would be fought on the land, in the air, and on the sea. Unleashing new technologies like tanks, aircrafts, and machine guns onto the battlefields meant soldiers and leaders had to adapt quickly or die. The old way of waging war was gone; the modern era had been born.

Although an assassination sparked the fighting, tensions had been simmering for a while, and pacts between these different countries forced them all into the war. Disagreements between Serbia and Austria came to a boiling point when the Austrian Archduke was shot in 1914. Instead of handling the issue, the dispute spilled over into war being declared. Within days, other major powers had been pulled into the fight.

The Allies were initially sent into panic, as the Germans pushed them back into France, until they changed tactics and managed to hold out against the pressure at the Battle of Marne. It was a major shift in what was supposed to be a short war and set the stage for a long, grueling trench war. Fought mainly on the frontlines of Europe, soldiers were stationed in trenches, waiting, firing shots at the enemy until one side was brave or reckless enough to charge against the other.

With intense battles fought at the Somme, Verdun, Ypres, and Meusse-Argonne, the fighting dragged on with victories and defeats for both sides until the United States came onto the scene. Bringing men and artillery with them, they helped to swing the direction of the war against the Germans in 1917. The following year would see the Allies defeat every final offensive against them and bring an end to the war with the signing of the Treaty of Versailles.

This book will not only give you the dates, facts, and figures, but it will also tell the fascinating stories of what really happened, giving you all the details of how the battles were fought, and highlighting the key players. After reading this, you will know:

INTRODUCTION

- The causes of the war and who was involved.
- The major battles and the turning points of the war, along with statistics and incredible stories of heroism.
- The new technology and weapons used in the war and the effects they had.
- What it was like to be a soldier in the trenches and what trench warfare was all about.
- What Winston Churchill was doing in this war.
- How General von Hindenburg won a major victory over Russia at Tannenberg in 1914.
- Why Woodrow Wilson kept America neutral during the first half of the war and why he finally stepped in from 1917 until the end.

Filled with awesome tales of heroism and bravery, you will be transported back into the middle of the First World War. Read about leaders who fought for peace, and those who only wanted more power and territory. Experience the victories and defeats as if you were on the battlefield with the soldiers.

Also, look out for these add-ons throughout the book with some incredible extra insights into the war:

AMAZING FACTS

Take a jump into the muddy trenches and find out everything you can about the war that changed the modern world!

1

WHAT CAUSED WORLD WAR 1?

Ask anyone how World War 1 began, and the answer is usually because an archduke got shot. It seems to be the perfect reason—revenge and retaliation. But the cause of the war is not as simple as one man and his wife being assassinated. There was much more happening behind the scenes and between the countries involved than that.

Europe did not explode into battle because of one man. The murder of a high-ranking political official was simply the perfect excuse to put into action what had already started long before that. It was the last block placed on an already badly-built tower of disagreements and division in Europe that was teetering on the edge of collapse.

Tensions had been mounting for years with nations taking sides over political issues. Mistrust had been brewing after a series of smaller conflicts, and while everyone tried their best to keep the peace and stick to their borders, there were those who were looking for a fight.

THE CONCERT OF EUROPE FALLS APART

In the early 1800s, the more powerful nations of Europe—Great Britain, Austria, Russia, Prussia, and France—began to write and sign a series of treaties to bring calm and stability to the region. After the Napoleonic Wars, they wanted to make sure no one could try to conquer lands and build an empire like that again. They also wanted to avoid internal uprisings like the French Revolution that would change the political system of a country.

It was a good idea to keep the peace, especially after so many wars had been fought. The Concert of Europe was an agreement between the most powerful of Europe's leaders to abide by a set of principles in their relations with one another (Lascurettes, 2017). At the Congress of Vienna in 1815, an agreement was made to keep the peace. For the first half of the 1800s, most European borders stayed the same and there was little in the way of major conflicts. The treaties seemed to be working.

But mounting tensions caused the alliance to shift, and the Austro-Prussian War, the Franco-Prussian War, and the Russo-Turkish War broke out causing diplomatic relations to fall apart. The biggest cause of concern though, was when Germany unified all its separate kingdoms into one very powerful nation in 1871. Otto von Bismarck very quickly turned what had been a number of independent states into one country. In a short amount of time, Germany rose as an industrial power looking to expand its military and prepare a much larger navy. This was a clear threat to those around it, especially Great Britain which saw the increasing number of surface ships being built as a challenge to its naval supremacy.

An arms race ensued where countries rushed to make sure they had enough weapons, soldiers, and ships in case of war. The strain of maintaining such a large army and navy was too much for Germany, and they tried diplomacy to ease the tension between them and Great Britain, but this was never anything but cheap talk. In the end, Germany stopped building ships and focused only on submarines, something that would become very effective against their enemies later during the war.

AMAZING FACT

- *Germany's massive navy only fought one real battle during World War 1—the Battle of Jutland—with no real winner!*

Added to this, Germany formed an alliance with its very large neighbor, Austria-Hungary. The second largest country at that time, Austria-Hungary reached across much of central-eastern Europe and had one of the biggest populations at that time. This coalition tipped the balance of power that other countries like Russia, Great Britain, and France enjoyed. The Concert of Europe was cracking under the pressure.

THE BALKAN POWDER KEG

The Balkans are often seen as one of the main reasons for causing the conflict to erupt. It's why it was called "the powder keg of Europe," because everything that happened there was like igniting the explosion that was just waiting to happen (Seaver, 2022).

The Ottoman Empire had ruled across much of southern Europe for over 600 years, but in the late 1800s, it began losing its influence over the region. The once-strong Turkish realm had suffered and become weak. Austria-Hungary saw a weakness and wasted no time in swooping in to claim their own prize by annexing Bosnia and Herzegovina in 1908, even though these were still part of the Ottoman Empire (Seaver, 2022). This move angered Russia and Serbia who already were not on friendly terms with Austria-Hungary. Italy also saw a chance to expand and invaded Ottoman-owned Libya, which increased tensions in the area.

The southeastern countries of Serbia, Bulgaria, Greece, and Montenegro now realized they had an opportunity to be free of Ottoman rule and began a war to break away. The First Balkan War in 1912-1913 was successful for these nations as they quickly overcame any Turkish resistance (Seaver, 2022). However, once they were victorious, another argument over who should get what escalated into the Second Balkan War. Former allies were suddenly fighting each other for the spoils of war! Bulgaria attacked Serbia and Greece but was defeated, leaving them humiliated and resentful.

It was in the middle of this chaos that someone decided that an assassination would be the best way to make a point. But instead, it proved to be the fuse that lit the powder keg!

THE ASSASSINATION OF THE ARCHDUKE

The man who pulled the trigger on June 28, 1914, was Gavrilo Princip, a Bosnian Serb nationalist. He was part of a secret group called Young Bosnia, which was armed by Black Hand whose aim was to unify the Bosnians, Slovenes, and Croats ruled by Austria-Hungary into a Greater Serb or south Slavic (Yugoslav) state (Guzvica, 2022). Only 19 years old at the time, Princip convinced others in the group that killing the Archduke would help end the Austria-Hungarian rule of Bosnia, which it had annexed in 1908.

Archduke Franz Ferdinand was the heir to the Austro-Hungarian throne and was traveling with his wife to Sarajevo as part of a state visit. For these young men, he seemed the perfect target. But the plans backfired, and Franz Ferdinand almost escaped the attempts on his life.

The first two men, who had a bomb with them, suddenly decided the time was not right as they watched the cars drive by. A third man threw a bomb at the open-topped car, but it bounced off and only detonated later, injuring many bystanders. The royal entourage sped off down the road past three more assassins, one of them Princip, all unable to do anything at that moment. The Archduke, his wife, and the Governor proceeded to the city hall for a reception. Afterward, they decided to continue with the tour.

In the end, it was the driver of the vehicle who presented them with their best chance. After not being given clear directions, he took a wrong turn and when he tried reversing, jammed the engine right in front of Princip who was standing outside Schiller's Delicatessen. The young man could not believe his luck, drew his gun, and shot the Archduke and his wife, Sophie. She died almost instantly while he was declared dead about half an hour later. Princip then turned the gun on himself but was wrestled to the ground before he could pull the trigger and was then arrested.

Too young to be given the death penalty, Princip was sentenced to prison for 20 years, but died of tuberculosis a few months before the end of World War 1.

AMAZING FACT

- The man who threw the bomb, Nedeljko Čabrinović, tried to commit suicide before being captured. He took a pill of cyanide and jumped off a bridge, but didn't succeed when he vomited the pill up and landed in water that was only knee-deep (Guzvica, 2022).

WAR DECLARATIONS

Austria-Hungary immediately assumed Serbia was behind the assassination and threw down an ultimatum that it knew the country would not be able to accept. It was the perfect chance to defeat their smaller neighbor once and for all. Knowing it had the backing of their German allies, Austria-Hungary declared war on July 28, 1914, and began bombing Belgrade, the capital of Serbia, the next day (Royde-Smith & Showalter, 2018).

Like a line of stacked dominoes, every other country was forced to quickly decide where they stood and who they supported, and one by one, they were all drawn into the war. Russia jumped to defend its ally, Serbia, and after warning Austria-Hungary not to attack Serbia, mobilized its army. This led to Germany declaring war on Russia, then France, and in a quick series of moves on August 3rd, its army pushed through Belgium to reach France.

This was the trigger for Great Britain to step in. It was not concerned with Serbia, the main cause of the whole disagreement in the first place, but it was sworn to protect Belgium. It was also looking to prevent a French defeat which would have left Germany in control of Western Europe. On August 4th, the King declared war after the expiration of an ultimatum to Germany. The dominoes fell quickly after that with every country taking sides and declaring war against anyone allied with their enemies. Japan joined the struggle on August 23rd by officially stating they were against Germany (Royde-Smith & Showalter, 2018).

Russia, Great Britain, and France secretly signed the Treaty of London, formally binding them together as the Allies versus the Central Powers of Austria-Hungary, Germany, and later Turkey. In the spirit of patriotism, most Europeans felt good about the war and accepted it, thinking it would be over in a few months. But no one had any idea that one assassination would lead to over four years of fighting and death.

2.

WHICH COUNTRIES TOOK PART IN THE WAR?

What made this different from other wars? Not just the new technology and weapons, but the vast territory it stretched across, from Europe to Africa and the Middle East. But the major contrast was the number of countries that took part. 32 nations declared war over the course of four years. Many of these were European, but others like Japan and the United States changed it from being a continental squabble into a full-blown world war.

Some chose not to get involved, and remained neutral. Others were forced in because they already had promised their allegiance to another country that was being picked on. There were others, like the United States, who were dragged in reluctantly when they became the targets of Germany's submarine warfare.

As in any war, there were two main sides: the Central Powers, which were the first to get the ball rolling by declaring war, and the Allies, who retaliated to the aggressive mobilization of armies and attacks. With far more countries on its side and more men to bring to the frontlines, the Allies outweighed their enemies by far.

In total, 60 million soldiers responded to the call to fight for their side, making it the largest manned war in history up to that date.

CENTRAL POWERS

This alliance is seen as the wrong side, probably because they were the first to declare war for their own selfish reasons, as well as the fact that they lost! They had all been looking to expand and grow their empires through force or manipulation and assumed they would be involved in small, short skirmishes rather than a drawn-out, worldwide war.

Four Main Players

Although Austria-Hungary was the largest in terms of size and people, it was Germany that took the lead in the war since it possessed the biggest army and the most weapons. After unifying all the smaller kingdoms within its region into one proud nation, it set about mobilizing a massive armed force which included amassing one of the largest navies at the time.

Not only was it looking to expand its borders, but it was worried about being trapped! With only one friendly neighbor to the south, Germany was sandwiched between two other countries it did not trust: France and Russia. Looking to assert itself and be fully prepared to fight, the plan was to knock out France quickly and then turn on Russia. This plan never worked because its actions triggered a war on both sides, not just one frontal attack as it hoped.

The Western and Eastern Fronts became the main areas where troops clashed. On the west, Germany fought France and Britain, while the east saw them tackle Russia. This put a strain on its large army as it was continually split, fighting a war on two fronts.

Austria-Hungary also had a point to prove. With its emperor, Francis Joseph, weak and dying, it needed to bolster its image as a great power in Europe and not be seen as a tired, fragile nation.

Looking to squash any Serbian resistance, fortify their borders, and show its strength, it declared war. It never would have done so if it had not been for the "blank check assurance" it was given by their closest ally, Germany (Norwich University Online, 2017). This pact to support each other no matter what gave Austria-Hungary the courage to make its moves.

The Ottoman Empire, meanwhile, had been one of the greatest kingdoms but it was on the decline. With the Balkan states revolting, it had taken a huge blow to its ego and borders. It was regarded as an outsider and was not actively involved in the start of the war. Initially, it was in discussions with both the Central Powers and the Allies, but seeing the advantages of gaining territory in Russia, it secretly formed an alliance with Germany on July 30, 1914 (Beck, 2017a). Rather than declare war itself, it tried to trick Russia into attacking, so it would have a legitimate reason for retaliating.

Bulgaria was not interested in getting involved and tried to remain neutral. But both the Central Powers and Allies tried to convince the country to join its side, and after seeing a chance for revenge for losing the Balkan Wars, it jumped in with the Central Powers.

AMAZING FACT

- *By the autumn of 1918, 900,000 Bulgarian men, nearly 40% of the male population, had been conscripted. The army suffered 300,000 casualties, including 100,000 killed, the most severe losses per head of any country involved in the war.*

ALLIED POWERS

The initial countries of this group were also known as the Triple Entente, three allies that signed the Treaty of London before the war broke out (Beck, 2021). These nations aligned their forces against what they saw as an aggressive attack on the sovereignty of other countries. For the most part, the Allies were not looking for ways to gain territory but were rather responding to the actions of the Central Powers, coming to the aid of their neighbors who were being targeted by Germany and Austria-Hungary. Later, other countries joined in forming a large Allied and Affiliates Force.

Three Key Countries

Great Britain only wanted to maintain the balance of power in Europe. It believed Germany's antagonistic movements would upset that with its large military and aggressive intentions. Since it had one of the biggest navies at that time, Britain saw its role as one of preventing the growing threat of German expansion. It was also committed to protecting Belgium, and once German forces entered its borders, there was no other choice but to declare war. From 1914 to 1918, Britain never changed its reason for fighting.

France recognized England as a friendly nation but shared a much closer alliance at that time with Russia. Because of this pact, it was seen as a threat to Germany. During the incidents and escalations that led to war being declared, instead of trying to find a peaceful solution, France backed its partner, Russia, and this put it firmly against the Central Powers and their objectives. With 3.5 million soldiers, it was positive about the prospect of going to war and winning quickly (Beck, 2021). However, it had to redefine its war policy as the fighting dragged on.

Russia was the largest country of all those involved, with the most people and the richest resources, but was so far behind in industrialization that it lacked a strong military presence and had a weak leadership under Tsar Nicholas II (Beck, 2021). Unlike its partners in the alliance, it had definite intentions of gaining more territory from fighting. Its strong support for Serbia set it against Austria-Hungary when war was declared. When the Ottomans joined in, Russia saw the chance to snap up land along the Mediterranean to increase its presence in the region.

Others Involved

At the signing of the peace treaty at the end of the war, there were 27 countries listed alongside the Allies. Some joined early on, with others being caught in the crossfire and compelled to step in. Many only joined toward the end once the US entered the fighting.

Japan's involvement may have been more of an opportunity to reap the benefits in the end, since no actual fighting took place in their country. It only suffered 2,000 casualties during the whole war, but its naval abilities and resources were used extensively to limit the Germans from dominating the seas (Kiilleen, 2017). As part of its previous alliance with Great Britain, Japan was quick to offer assistance.

AMAZING FACT

- *The Japanese defeat of German forces at Tsingtao was the first time seaplanes were used to sink a German minelayer and attack strategic positions (Kiilleen, 2017).*

Italy was initially aligned with Austria-Hungary and Germany, but when war broke out, it declared itself neutral. It eventually decided to enter on the side of the Allies, a move that opened up a new frontier and also weakened the capabilities of the Central Powers.

Belgium, Greece, Montenegro, Romania, and Serbia all threw their support to the Allies. Although their combined force of 1.5 million soldiers was heavily involved in many of the battles, the decision-making and control always laid in the hands of the Triple Entente (Beck, 2021).

The USA was another late arrival to the war. Its reluctance to enter was backed by Woodrow Wilson, the president, but he saw it as the American's duty to support the war effort by providing resources and funding. Although the soldiers it sent only arrived in 1917, it was perfect timing since Russia had to pull out due to the civil unrest back in its own country. The 4.3 million US reinforcements were also fresh and keen to fight, not having been bogged down in the trenches that dominated the first half of WW1 (Beck, 2021). Its involvement swung the direction of the war in the Allies' favor.

There were numerous others that fought out of loyalty, especially those belonging to the British Empire, such as Canada, Australia, New Zealand, South Africa, and India, who all signed up to fight under the British crown.

3

LEADERS AND GENERALS

In every war there are soldiers waiting in trenches, charging at the enemy, or dying on the frontlines. But they are just "boots on the ground!" Even though they give their lives to fight, the outcome is usually determined by one or two men making all the critical decisions. Victory or defeat rests with generals strategizing the finer points on a map, and maneuvering artillery, ships, and infantry—they are the masterminds of the battle.

But even they do not always determine the war itself. Far from the mud, death, and smell of gunfire, there are leaders in offices, using their political influence to steer events toward their own end.

These are the men with the power to change the direction and the result of a war.

ALLIED POLITICAL LEADERS AND MILITARY GENERALS

Great Britain

David Lloyd George

From 1914 to 1915, Lloyd George was the minister of munitions, which meant he was in charge of bombs, bullets, and explosives. Despite fierce resistance, he pushed through a bold, unorthodox move to increase the production of these items. In 1916, when the Battle of the Somme began, there was no shortage of supplies because of Lloyd George's efforts (Blake & Blake, 2019).

When he came into office as prime minister in 1916, he immediately changed the way the war office operated, allowing room for quicker decisions to be made and enforced. His major contribution was tackling the German submarine problem which was causing food shortages. Lloyd George ensured the convoy system was put in place where warships sailed with merchant vessels. He also stepped up agricultural production to make sure Britain did not starve.

But his war efforts were not as good and he was always in disagreement with Haig and Kitchener, almost costing them key battles. In the end, the war was successful, and Lloyd George's diplomacy helped steer the Treaty of Versailles from being even more heavy-handed than it was.

Lord Horatio Kitchener

A decorated officer, Kitchener was named Baron of Khartoum for his efforts in Sudan (Roller, 2021). He then led the army in the Second Boer War in South Africa where he introduced the successful, but controversial, "scorched earth policy."

Kitchener's face on recruitment poster

In his post overseeing WW1, he was one of the only people who believed it would not be a short clash, but a long, drawn-out affair, and warned everyone to prepare for it. He is credited with transforming the British army into a modern unit, for inspiring millions to sign up in 1914, and even including his face on the recruitment poster (Roller, 2021).

His involvement in the Gallipoli Campaign and the Shell Crisis was disastrous, but he still was generally admired. On June 5, 1916, he was aboard the HMS *Hampshire* on his way to discuss tactics with Tsar Nicholas II, when it struck a German mine, killing him and 736 others (Roller, 2021).

Field Marshall Sir Douglas Haig

Haig was put in charge of the BEF (British Expeditionary Force), the largest unit the UK had ever put into the field. His methods of winning cost the lives of many soldiers as he believed in a war of attrition, where the longer you fought, more of the enemy died! At the Somme (1916) and Passchendaele (1917), he suffered huge losses, stubbornly holding out long after it was clear no victory could be won.

However, by 1918 he began using the "All Arms" strategy of combining tanks, artillery, infantry, cavalry, and air power into attacks with incredible effect during the Hundred Days War ("Douglas Haig: The chief", 2000).

Haig used his words well to inspire the men, and one of his most famous was the "Backs to the Wall" communique, where he said (Duffy, 2009a):

Many amongst us now are tired. To those I would say that victory will belong to the side which holds out the longest. The French Army is moving rapidly and in great force to our support. There is no other course open to us but to fight it out. Every position must be held to the last man: there must be no retirement. With our backs to the wall and believing in the justice of our cause each one of us must fight on to the end. (para.4)

AMAZING FACT

- The BEF was the most well-trained European force with the average soldier being able to hit a target 300 yards away 15 times in a minute with a Lee-Enfield Rifle (Higgins, n.d.).

Winston Churchill

Churchill spearheaded the Dardanelles expedition, which he saw as a way to break the stalemate that was happening on the Western Front at that time. The naval attack failed, and Churchill was blamed, leading him to resign from the government and go and fight on the frontlines as an officer instead. He later returned to politics where he was appointed as the minister of munitions by Lloyd George.

Russia

Tsar Nicholas II

Not in favor of going to war, Nicholas tried diplomacy to avoid a full mobilization of troops against the Central Powers. But his popularity was taking a dive among his own people and after taking over command of the army, things became worse. With little knowledge of war, the empress and Rasputin had a certain power to make decisions that only angered the public even more. On July 16, 1918, he was deposed and executed by the Bolsheviks, ending the Romanov Dynasty (Keep, 2019)

Aleksey Brusilov

The commander of the South-West Front of the Imperial Russian Army became famous for what was known as the Brusilov Offensive. After a number of defeats, Brusilov used the element of surprise by moving his army and artillery as far forward as possible before firing at the enemy to break holes into the frontline. As a result, he moved 30 km forward, taking 400,000 prisoners as he advanced, one of the most successful maneuvers of the war

("Russia Attacks", n.d.). This solved the problem of how to attack trenches.

France

Georges Clemenceau

As the leader of France, he called for soldiers to enlist when the war broke out, as well as pushing for more guns and ammunition for his troops. He also sent many appeals to Woodrow Wilson for America to join the war. He was focused on victory at all costs and had no time for traitors or cowards. He is most famous for saying that his country would fight "to the last quarter hour, for the last quarter hour will be ours" (Monnerville, 1998, para. 3).

He was the harshest critic of Germany in the end, wanting them to pay the highest price for their part in the war. As one of the significant powers, Clemenceau helped set the terms of the Treaty of Versailles.

General Joseph Joffre

Known as the "Silent General", Joffre led the French forces on the Western Front. He was most famous for his role in organizing the retreating French forces and then leading them to victory in the First Battle of the Marne ("Joseph Joffre", n.d.).

Ferdinand Foch

A key French military leader, Foch was always optimistic, sometimes to the detriment of his soldiers when he did not know when to pull back or stop attacking. He had a stunning victory at the First Battle of the Marne, but then suffered some disastrous decisions and was replaced. However, he was brought back toward the end of the war as leader of the Allied Forces, withstanding the Ludendorff Offensive and breaking down the Germans until they could no longer fight. He oversaw the details of the armistice Germany was forced to sign on a railway carriage.

Philippe Pétain

The "Hero of Verdun," Pétain was organized, methodical, and looked after his troops. Although the situation at Verdun was hopeless, he brought order into the chaos and inspired heroism in his men. Under his direction, the French troops were successful in helping Ferdinand Foch's offensive of 1918.

Philippe Pétain

Italy

Victor Emmanuel III

The Italian government wanted to stay out of the war, but King

Victor ignored their protests and joined in with the Allies. He had his eye on gaining some territory from Austria-Hungary. However, the Italian army was riddled with corruption and so disorganized that they suffered significant defeats. As a result, the country went through a severe economic depression.

Vittorio Orlando

Prime Minister from 1917, Orlando brought some optimism after the Italian army suffered a heavy defeat at Caporetto. As a strong supporter of the war, he held the secret deals of more territory promised by the Allies in the Treaty of London 1915. But when he faced opposition to his demands at the Paris Peace Conference, he walked out of negotiations.

Belgium

King Albert I

As King of Belgium, he rejected the ultimatum from Germany to give it free passage through his country to get to France, and as a result, Belgium was invaded in 1914 (Tikkanen, 2019). Albert assumed leadership of the army once the Germans entered Belgium, but he had to retreat when the enemy's forces proved too strong. Germany ended up occupying most of the country for the entire war. During this time, Albert remained with his soldiers, visiting them on the front lines.

United States

Woodrow Wilson

America remained out of the war because of President Wilson's belief that his country should remain neutral. However, he did make sure that support in the way of resources and funds was made available. It wasn't until 1917, when Germany increased its submarine attacks on merchant ships, that the United States had little choice but to retaliate. Wilson persuaded his government to join the war effort.

He was an important figure in the peace negotiations at the end of the war, even pushing for his idea of a League of Nations to be adopted.

Here are two of his most famous sayings about the war:

"This is a war to end all wars."
-Published in The Daily News on Aug. 14, 1914 (Choi, 2017, para. 1).

"I can predict with absolute certainty that within another generation there will be another world war if the nations of the world do not concert the method by which to prevent it"
-From a speech given at Omaha in 1919 after the war ("How President Woodrow Wilson", 2018, para. 7).

General John Pershing

Nicknamed "Black Jack" or known by the soldiers as "Lord God Almighty," Pershing was a legendary officer who struck fear into those under his command. He was Wilson's choice to head up the AEF (Allied Expeditionary Force) when the US entered the war in 1917. However, his first few months were spent fighting the Germans and filling in gaps in the British and French armies with reinforcements. Pershing began operating on his own, with his own troops and made a huge impact pushing back the Germans at Catigny, Chateau-Thierry, and St. Mihiel ("John J. Pershing", 2018).

AMAZING FACT

- Douglas McArthur, who would go on to play a major role in WW2, was under Pershing's command during WW1 and impressed his commander as a second lieutenant.

CENTRAL POWERS POLITICAL LEADERS AND MILITARY GENERALS

Germany

Kaiser Wilhelm II

The German emperor (Kaiser) and King of Prussia, he came to the throne when he was 29 years old. His lack of diplomacy was evident in his comments and actions. When Paul Kruger defeated the British-led Jameson Raid in South Africa in 1896, Wilhelm congratulated him (Balfour, 2019), which angered the British. He also denied that Germany was challenging control of the seas, even though his country was building a bigger navy.

Although he was the supreme commander of Germany during the war, he allowed his generals and politicians to make the decisions, supporting them in not negotiating peace. At the end of WW1, he was forced to abdicate the throne and went to live in exile in the Netherlands (Balfour, 2019).

AMAZING FACT

- As eldest grandchild of Britain's Queen Victoria, Wilhelm was a cousin of the British King George V. King George was also a cousin of Tsar Nicholas, making all three related. Wilhelm and Nicholas referred to each other as "Willy" and "Nicky," even *when writing to each other, which makes it sound even more mad that we had a war (The Kaiser", n.d.)!*

Erich Ludendorff

Ludendorff was very active and called for a stronger army, which at first irritated the authorities, who demoted him to a lesser role. However, when it looked like Russia was going to conquer the 8th Army, he was appointed secondary commander under General von Hindenburg. Together, they pulled off a surprise victory at the Battle of Tannenberg in 1914 but experienced a huge defeat straight after that at Marne (Gorlitz, 2019).

Hindenburg, Kaiser Wilhelm, and Ludendorff

By 1917, he and von Hindenburg had been given total power of the army, and in effect, made decisions for the whole of Germany, even trying to find a replacement leader for the country. Ludendorff gave the submarines the go-ahead to increase their attacks, which led to the United States entering the war. On March 21, 1918, he also tried an unsuccessful last push against the Western Front to smash the

Allies before the Americans arrived, but it was a failure (Gorlitz, 2019).

In the end, he resigned but always claimed that his plans had been sabotaged by his own people.

Paul von Hindenburg

Not easily shaken, von Hindenburg assumed leadership of the German Army and won fame for the victory at Tannenberg. He became a war hero for his role in the wars on the Eastern Front but failed to bring about the same results when he went to the Western Front. When it was clear that Germany was looking at defeat, he let Ludendorff take all the blame.

He later became president of the country, running for a second term against a very aspiring Adolf Hitler.

Austria-Hungary

Emperor-King Franz Joseph I

As ruler of Austria-Hungary for 68 years, he held huge influence over the region. He relied on his friendships with other sovereigns to keep the peace, but by the early 1900s, had few relationships with other kings or emperors to hold on to, except Wilhelm II of Germany. Despite his belief in peace, he was persuaded to issue an ultimatum to Serbia in 1914, which set off a chain of war declarations. He died before the end of the war.

Emperor-King Karl I

Assuming the throne after Joseph I died, he immediately set about trying to secretly negotiate peace deals through his brother-in-law, but these were dismissed by France. He tried to bring changes to the Austro-Hungarian army, but it was too late since his country relied heavily on Germany for military support. Toward the end of the war, he again tried to find a peaceful solution, but it was all for nothing. In the end, he was forced to abdicate, and his empire was dismantled.

Ottoman Empire

Enver Pasha

As minister of war, he negotiated a military alliance with both Germany and Russia, finally joining the Central Powers after Russia rejected the proposals. His first command of the Third Army was a complete disaster, suffering a humiliating defeat at Sarikamis on December 29, 1914 (Duffy, 2009c). However, he had a part in the significant victory at the Dardanelles. When the war ended, he fled to Germany and then Russia.

4

WORLD WAR 1 IN NUMBERS

There had never been a war like this one. The number of soldiers and weapons exceeded anything that had been before. Countries threw everything they had into the battles that stretched on for days, months, and years. Not only was this war bigger but there were more new additions like planes, tanks, and submarines that had not been seen in wars fought previously. The financial cost was shocking, but the cost of lives was far more devastating!

OUTRAGEOUS NUMBERS

- **32**

Nations involved in the war (Bishop, n.d.)

- **65 million**

Soldiers that took part in the war

- **9.7 million**

Deaths of soldiers in battle

- **10 million**

Deaths of civilians

- **8 million**

Horses killed in action

- **6 million**

Prisoners of war

- **1.5 billion**

Explosive shells fired on the Western Front

- **220,000**

Aircraft produced for the war

- **7,700**

Tanks produced for the war (Germany only made 20!)

- **5,000**

Ships lost at sea from U-boat attacks

- $186 billion ($334 billion equivalent today)

Total cost of the war (Bishop, n.d.)

STARTLING AMOUNTS

- 12

How old Sydney Lewis was when he joined the army—he lied about his age ("32 interesting facts", 2020).

- 2 billion

Letters delivered to the soldiers on the frontline by the time the war ended (Bishop, n.d.).

- 35,000 miles

The entire length of trenches dug during the war ("First trenches", 2009).

- 140 miles

An explosive blowing up in Belgium could be heard that far away in London (Lehnardt, 2016).

- 1 third

Number of military deaths caused by the Spanish Flu.

- 11/11/11

The Armistice was signed at 11 am on 11th November 1918 (Lehnardt, 2016).

- 500,000

Pigeons used to carry messages between headquarters and the frontlines (Andreajn, 2019).

- **5ft 3ins**

The minimum height required to serve in the British Army, but "bantam battalions" were created for those who were shorter than that (Lang, 2014).

- **1 minute**

Henry Gunther was killed 60 seconds before the Armistice was announced, making him the last soldier killed in action ("32 interesting facts", 2020).

- **90%**

The percentage of the 7.8 million soldiers from Austria-Hungary who fought in the war that were either injured or killed ("32 interesting facts", 2020).

- 14

The age of Private John Condon, who was the youngest Allied soldier killed, who died in a gas attack during the Second Battle of Ypres in 1915 (Furbank, 2018).

DEADLY FIGURES

The number of soldiers killed and wounded in war is important as it gives an idea of the scale of each battle. Instead of glorifying the conflict, it should be a shocking reminder of how many lives were lost. In WW1, many men died as a result of bad decisions or not understanding the changing method of fighting wars in the modern era.

1. **Hundred Days Offensive** – August 1918

   1,855,369 casualties
   The Germans were defeated which resulted in the peace treaty.
   Germans 785,733, Allies 1,069,636 (incl. 127,000 Americans)
("The 10 Bloodiest Battles", 2023)

2. **The Spring Offensive** – March 1918

   1,539,715 casualties
   The Allies halted the advance of the German troops.
   Germans 680,000, Allies 850,000

3. **Battle of the Somme** – July 1916

1,219,201 casualties
   The Somme is an example of the senseless slaughters of the war.
   19,240 British soldiers were killed on the 1st day!
   Germans 800,000, Allies 623,906

4. Battle of Verdun – February 1916

976,000 casualties
   Over 40 million artillery shells fired during the battle.
   Germans 435,000, French 542,000

5. The Battle of Passchendaele

   848,614 casualties
   Part of the Third battle of Ypres, in Flanders, Belgium. Miserable conditions with both sides suffering major casualties. The British only gained small territorial gains for their efforts.
   Germans 400,000, Allies 448,614

6. The Serbian Campaign – July 1914

   633,500 casualties
   A series of battles between Austria-Hungary and Serbia. During the whole war, Serbian losses equaled 27% of its total population and 60% of its male population.

7. The First Battle of the Marnes – September 1914

   483,000 casualties
   The battle that ended the German invasion of France and led to trench warfare.
   Germans 220,000, Allies 263,000

8. The Gallipoli Campaign – February 1915

   473,000 total casualties
   The Allies hoped to break the deadlock on the Western Front

and relieve the Russians by opening up a sea route for resupply, but it ended in disaster.

Turks 253,000, Allies 220,000

9. Battle of Arras – April 1917

278,000 total casualties

The Western Front was a stalemate for two years with both sides suffering millions of casualties because of Verdun and the Somme. The Allies planned to attack the trenches at the town of Arras. It was a tactical British victory but wasn't the breakthrough they had hoped for.

Germans 120,000, Allies 158,000

10. Battle of Tannenberg – August 1914

182,000 total casualties

A decisive victory for the Germans, being outnumbered by two Russian field armies, they decimated the second army and almost the whole of the first army.

Russians 170,000, Germans 12,000 ("The 10 Bloodiest Battles", 2023)

5

TACTICS AND TECHNOLOGY

World War 1 changed the face of fighting. It turned the way wars had been fought upside down. The old way of staring down an opposing force on the frontlines had disappeared. New technology meant adapting to new ways to defend and attack. You could be killed without even knowing your enemy had you in their sights! But generals were slow to learn these lessons, and it cost thousands of lives as they fumbled with their strategies, trying to combat the new weapons against them. The soldiers following these outdated commands were like "lions being led by donkeys" (Budnik, 2019, para.1).

CHANGING TACTICS

Uniforms and Soldiers

It might be strange, even comical, to think that officers still had swords strapped to their sides and rode horses into battle when machine guns and tanks were also on the frontlines. Even worse, many of the soldiers wore cloth caps and had bayonets on the end of their rifles in the belief that close combat was still the way to fight.

Many of these ideas had to change to keep up with the speed and ferocity of how warfare was being conducted. The British had learned this the hard way back in the Boer Wars when they trudged across in their bright red blazers like targets for the enemy to pick off. This time, they entered the war wearing khaki, the color the Boers had used so effectively against them. The Germans had adopted a neutral grey which was very effective. The French, however, were a lot slower to transform from their outdated Napoleonic uniforms. They entered the war in blue tunics and red trousers, with their officers wearing white gloves (Fowler, n.d.). They soon changed all of this to become less obvious on the battlefield.

Along with these changes, in 1908 the British introduced webbed pouches and ammunition belts to carry their heavy loads and became more mobile in the field (Fowler, n.d.). But the kit they had to carry still weighed over 70 pounds! Victor Packer of the Royal Irish Fusiliers said (Fowler, n.d.):

You still had in those days, a full pack, 250 rounds of ammunition, water bottle, haversack, rifle, bayonet, and often you carried a bit of something extra as well. We were daft enough to carry souvenirs in those days like nose caps of shells and things or a Uhlan's helmet, whatever we could get like that we prized, but not long afterwards we threw them over a hedge or somewhere (para. 5).

There were a lot of changes made to equip the soldiers to be able to move quickly and fight smarter. Even the height of normal boots was altered to shorter ones with cloth wraparounds to keep out the dirt and stones. Metal helmets were introduced which saved many men from fatal headwounds.

Helmet saves head from shrapnel

Instead of what was initially a colonial police force to stop any small revolts or uprisings before the war, the British Army quickly became a much larger unit filled with civilians who knew very little about the war. The massive scale of managing such a large force was new to officers, and it was only by late 1917, after some tough lessons, that soldiers and generals were fighting more efficiently and strategically.

Strategies

The way to win a war had always been one of attrition—attacking for as long as possible to wear the other side down, hoping for a breakthrough. Large-scale artillery barrages were always followed by a slow advance of the entire unit of soldiers. This way of attacking was drawn-out and always ended in a huge loss of life. Many of the generals in WW1 had come from fighting battles this way, and so they assumed it would work again.

Against trenches and modern technology, these tactics proved costly! World War 1 has often been described as a "pointless bloodbath" ("Tactics in warfare", 2022). But, it also brought about a paradigm shift—a new way of looking at and doing things. Generals had to change their mindsets. Some took longer to do this than others.

Horses had been so effective as cavalry before, but navigating the deadly crisscross of the dugouts and barbed wire strung across the Western Front ruled them out of any attack. Even though armored vehicles were around, they were cumbersome, not easy to drive, or able to move swiftly through muddy terrain. When soldiers managed to break through the defenses, moving back up to those positions was too slow and any chance of surprise turned into retreat or defeat. The trenches caused a stalemate, where the defensive choice to hold position seemed to be the best while those in charge figured out a better way of winning the war.

World War 1 caused strategists to look at things differently, and toward the end of the fighting, there were three major paradigm shifts in how the war would be fought from that moment on

1. Machines not men.

Battles were no longer about soldiers' and horses' muscles, but now focused on machines. The cavalry no longer dominated the frontline, and men could not outrun bullets! With the invention of the combustion engine, tanks, trucks, and vehicles began to dominate battlefields.

This change in mindset can best be seen in someone like General Haig who led the disastrous Passchendaele and Somme attacks, where he committed his men to a war of attrition instead of stopping and using other methods. Later, he encouraged the development of the tanks, seeing that they could have a very effective role in the war if used correctly.

2. Three-dimensional war.

War had always been fought on a flat plane of land and sea, but with the invention of the aircraft, everything changed. Suddenly, soldiers had to keep looking up for any chance of attack as well as in front and behind. Control of the skies was a completely new idea for generals to deal with.

The battle at Amiens in 1918 is a perfect example of how the Allies had modernized their approach from the Somme two years before and overran the Germans with swift, decisive attacks using both aircraft and land invasions (Sheffield, 2011).

Added to this, the oceans also became three-dimensional with the entrance of the submarine into World War 1. Instead of just scanning the horizon, admirals and captains now had to worry about what was underneath the water as well. Battleships that had ruled the seas for so long were like sitting ducks from above and below!

3. Deeper frontlines.

The most vulnerable had always been those standing facing the enemy, but once planes became a part of the war, it became clear that everyone was a target no matter where they were in the battle. The middle and rear of the army were just as exposed, and strategies needed to change to meet these new threats.

Before 1914, it had been like playing a normal game of chess, but then it suddenly changed into a multi-dimensional one where you needed to move 10 pieces at a time to keep up! War became more complicated, like a machine with many moving parts.

JAMES BURROWS

NEW TECHNOLOGIES

Tanks

This new innovation had mixed results in the war. Originally called "landships" and later named "tanks" because of how much they looked like large water tanks, they were more of a hazard than a help ("32 interesting facts", 2020). The early versions were difficult to drive, needed huge crews to operate, and were not as effective as was hoped.

Mark V Tank

Introduced by the British at the Somme in 1916, these large machines on tracks were briefly successful, but made little impact on the battle and ended up killing more of their own soldiers than the enemy (Zabecki, 2015). The French tried again later but got stuck trying to get them through the difficult terrain. As a result, German General Ludendorff saw little use for the technology, except to squash and bash through defenses. The Germans ended up only producing 20 of their own tanks compared to the Allies'

7,000. Instead, they put their minds to developing anti-tank measures which proved very successful in battle.

As a new addition, the tank would only really make its mark later when it appeared as a faster and more dangerous weapon in WW2.

AMAZING FACT

- *British tanks were referred to as male if they had 6-pounder cannons, and female if they were only armed with machine guns ("32 interesting facts", 2020).*

Machine Guns

One of the most successful inventions to change the face of war was the rapid-firing gun. The rifle had transformed from the days of having to reload after each and every shot. In 1883, Hiram Maxim developed his first automatic firearm, and by 1914, a number of manufacturers were producing different guns using small-caliber, smokeless cartridges (Cornish, 2015). It was one of the main reasons that WW1 became a trench war because soldiers could no longer rush at the enemy without getting mowed down by a spray of bullets.

Different tactics were used, such as grouping machine guns together at Loos on September 26, 1915, or on the Somme on July 1, 1916, and concentrating firepower on the enemy with destructive results (Cornish, 2015). But as newer, lighter versions like the Lewis Gun became available, others saw the chance for soldiers to become more mobile. Armed with machine guns and grenades, these small troops began to perfect a more flexible strategy of attacking.

Flamethrowers

The Germans brought this weapon into the war and used it more effectively than any other army. Under the command of Landwehr officer Bernhard Reddemann, the flamethrower was used first used at Malancourt on February 26, 1915, to shock the enemy (Cornish, 2016). At Verdun, they were very successful and Reddemann was given his own unit specifically trained to use these weapons. Other countries experimented and used flamethrowers, but never as much and as well as the Germans.

They were most damaging when used to "flush out" or "exterminate" soldiers from the trenches without damaging the structures. Burning the enemy alive brought a new terror to the war that generals had to find ways to neutralize or use.

Air Support

Sopwith Camel plane

Taking to the air was a new way of fighting, and balloons and Zeppelins became common sights over battlefields during the war. Mainly used to spy on enemy formations or to drop bombs on strategic locations, the skies became a new frontline. But it was the plane that completely changed the way battles were fought. Only 15 years after the Wright brothers made their first successful flight, flying aircraft were introduced into war for the first time.

Many of them were simple compared with later models and were initially only used for observing the enemy and reporting back. Once they were fitted with weapons, planes became lethal fighters. In 1917, the Junkers J-1 was first seen, a German plane armed with three machine guns and a bomb load (Zabecki, 2015). Although the Allies had double the number of aircraft, the Germans used their ground artillery successfully against them.

AMAZING FACT

- *The most successful fighter pilot was the Red Baron. Manfred Albrecht Freiherr von Richthofen was a German pilot who shot down 80 planes. He died after his plane was brought down near Amiens in 1918 (Lehnardt, 2016).*
- *The term "dogfight" was used to describe planes fighting each other. The name came from pilots turning the engine off so it would not stall when they turned the planes quickly in the air. When the engine restarted in midair, it sounded like dogs barking (Lascurettes, 2017).*

Poison Gas

Gas masks became a normal part of the war as each country experimented with chemical weapons. Although the Hague Peace Conference of 1899 tried to discourage the use of gas attacks, it was employed by both sides (Faith, 2016). The fear of what it could do was probably more powerful than the small number of soldiers it actually killed. It became a psychological advantage. As a weapon, it was not as effective as planned since the weather conditions had to be perfect, with the wind blowing the right way, no rain, and the method of delivery was unreliable.

The French tried tear gas while the Germans used chlorine gas on unsuspecting Allies at Ypres on April 22, 1915 (Faith, 2016). Phosgene killed more people in WW1 than others, but it was mustard gas that struck fear into most soldiers as it hung around in the air long after being deployed causing skin blisters on anyone who came near, even days later. 30 different types of gas were used, killing about 91,000 people (Lehnardt, 2016). In the end, all the countries signed treaties outlawing chemical warfare.

Tracer Bullets

The invention of tracer bullets revolutionized night warfare. Instead of firing away in the dark hoping to hit something, a soldier could now see the flight of their shots. Filled with flammable material at the base, it allowed the shooter to adjust their aim, and it became an effective way of taking out the German Zeppelins that were terrorizing the English night skies with their bombs.

AMAZING FACT

- *Women had to work in ammunition factories while the men became soldiers. Those who handled shells filled with TNT (an explosive compound) were called "Canary Girls" because their skin and hair turned yellow from exposure to the chemical (Potts & Rimmer, 2017).*

Wireless Communication

Signals office

The transition from old ways to modern technology is best seen in the area of communication. WW1 still saw runners, dogs, and pigeons being used to send messages between headquarters and the frontline. At the same time, troops were doing their best to take advantage of recent breakthroughs in wireless telegraphy. Britain still relied on telephones while the Germans were erecting wireless towers throughout their region. When the Allied telephone cables were destroyed in the Somme 1916, the British saw how effective wireless was and began investing more in new technology.

The use of Morse code at the beginning of the war slowly gave way to the radio toward the end, which was proving more and more of a game changer in the field. With so many countries sending strategic plans across the airwaves, armies began seeing the need for people who understood the technology to intercept these messages. The Germans gained critical information on the

Russian tactics at the Battle of Tannenberg in 1914 this way (Tikkanen, 2019).

AMAZING FACT

- *The job of runners was so dangerous that sometimes three were given the same message just to make sure at least one got across open ground under enemy fire to deliver it. Private James Miller was a runner during the Somme, and on July 30, 1916, he delivered his last message. He was shot in the back leaving the trench, but he held the gaping wound closed, delivered his message, staggered back with his answer, and fell dead once he delivered it (Cox, 2020).*

Mobile X-Ray Machines

Marie Curie may be best known as the discoverer of radium and polonium with regards to radioactivity, but she also developed the first x-ray machines that could be transported. This helped doctors to be able to diagnose problems close to the frontlines instead of patients having to be transported miles away to the nearest hospital.

To solve the problem of electricity, Curie installed a dynamo into each of the cars which became known as "Little Curies," first used at the Battle of Marne in 1914 (Jorgensen, 2017). Operators were trained and sent out as close to the battlefield as possible to help assess the damage to wounded soldiers.

X-ray room at Kitchener Hospital

6

TIMELINE OF THE WAR

There are many battles across a number of regions, and it can become confusing without a clear idea of how World War 1 progressed. Who was involved, how many died, and who won each battle, are all important questions, but rather than getting bogged down in the trenches like one of the soldiers not knowing what's going on, it's good to see a timeline of events. Just highlighting the main events will help to understand the war as you have a complete overview before getting into the specifics of each fight.

Already having looked at the reasons behind the countries getting involved, this timeline will start with the trigger that set it all off: the assassination of the archduke.

1914

June 28: The archduke was assassinated

Gavrilo Princip shoots and kills Archduke Franz Ferdinand, the heir to the Austro-Hungarian throne.

July 28: Austria-Hungary declared war on Serbia

Aug 1: Germany declared war on Russia

Aug 3: Germany declared war on France

Germany wanted to get to France and decided the only route was to go through Belgium. After asking permission to send troops through the country, and being denied, Germany launched an attack by sending troops into Belgium.

Aug 4: Germany invaded Belgium

Britain declared war

Because Germany invaded a country that Britain had sworn to defend, it had no choice but to stick to its promise and declared war on Germany. Canada joined in by also declaring war on the Central Powers.

The US decided not to get involved and Woodrow Wilson declared it would remain neutral.

Aug 5: The Battle of Liege

The first battle of the war, considered a moral victory for the Allies, as the heavily outnumbered Belgians held out against the German Army for 12 days.

Aug 10: Austria-Hungary invaded Russia

Aug 14: Battle of the Frontiers began

The first great clashes on the Western Front. All the first battles fought along the eastern border of France and in southern Belgium that resulted in a series of German victories and Allied retreats.

Aug 23: Japan declared war on Germany

Aug 26-30: Battle of Tannenberg

Russia attacks Germany along East Prussia (Poland). At first, the Russians have the upper hand, but when the Germans intercept tactical messages, they force the opposition to retreat ("World War I battles", 2021).

Sept 6-12: 1st Battle of Marne

The French and British manage to stop German forces from entering Paris 30 miles from the city ("World War I battles", 2021). The Germans move their army back to Aisne and the trench war begins.

Nov 3: Russia declared war on Ottoman Empire

Nov 5: Britain and France declared war on Ottoman Empire

Oct–Nov: 1st Battle of Ypres

Trying to win a "race to the sea" and control a strategic port in Belgium, the Germans and Allies get stuck in a trench war that ends with no winner as both sides call it off because of the harsh winter ("World War I battles", 2021).

Dec 8: Battle of Falkland Islands

British Navy warships destroy the German squadron of Admiral Graf von Spee in the South Atlantic off the coast of Argentina. Von Spee and two of his sons serving in his squadron are killed.

Dec 24-25: A Christmas Truce was called

1915

Jan 24: Battle of Dogger Bank

The British intercept enemy messages and go after a German squadron, sinking their cruiser.

Jan 31: Poison gas used for the first time

Feb 4: Germans blockaded Britain with submarines

Feb-Jan 1916: Battle of Gallipoli

The first beach landing saw the British and French try to rush in and take Constantinople from the Turks. What was supposed to be a quick victory turned out to be a long-drawn-out defeat as the Allies were forced to withdraw after losing too many men.

March 11: Britain blockaded German ports
April-May: 2nd Battle of Ypres

The first successful German attack with poison gas. However, they failed to use their advantage and in the end, both sides maintained their lines and advanced no further.

May 7: German submarine sunk the Lusitania

The first passenger liner to be hit killing many civilians on board.

May 23: Italy joined the war

June–Nov 1917: Battles of the Isonzo

A series of 12 battles fought between Italy and Austria-Hungary along the Isonzo River. After short, intense attacks, very little headway was made by the Italians, and they were finally pushed back.

Oct 14: Bulgaria entered the war

1916

Feb–Dec: Battle of Verdun

The longest battle of WW1, Germany launched a surprise attack against the French that left many dead on both sides. Although the Germans made significant advances at first, they were forced to pull out as the Brusilov Offensive on the Eastern Front meant their troops needed reinforcements.

Apr 29: Siege of Kut

British forces surrender to Turkish forces at Kut, Mesopotamia (modern day Iraq) after a five-month siege.

May–June: Battle of Jutland

The only major naval battle of WW1 ends with no real winner.

June–Aug: Brusilov Offensive

The largest and most successful Allied assault belonged to Russia. Using surprise and numbers, Brusliov ordered a full-scale attack that almost brought Austria-Hungary to its knees. It also forced the Central Powers to give up the land they had taken from Russia and pull more troops from wars being fought in the West to stop the Russian attack on the Eastern Front.

July–Nov: 1st Battle of the Somme

One of the bloodiest battles as British troops are cut down trying to run at the German trenches near the Somme River. Although the Allies changed their tactics, there are no real breakthroughs.

1917

Mar 15: Tsar Nicholas II abdicates

After the Russian Revolution, the tsar steps down and a provisional government is established. Great Britain, France, the United States, and Italy quickly recognize the new government so Russia might stay in the war on the Eastern Front.

April 6: America declared war on Germany

After German submarines continued attacking ships and the

Zimmerman telegram Germany sent to Mexico encouraging them to attack the US, Woodrow Wilson convinces his country to join the war.

May 19: Russia stays in the war

The Provisional Government of Russia announces it will stay in the war. A large offensive for the Eastern Front is planned by Alexander Kerensky, the new Minister of War. However, many Russian soldiers and peasants join Lenin's Bolshevik Party which opposes the war and the government.

May 27-June 1: French soldiers mutiny

French soldiers refuse orders to advance, angry over the battles of attrition and terrible living conditions in the muddy, rat and lice-infested trenches. The new Commander-in-Chief, Henri Petain, cracks down on the mutiny through mass arrests and firing squad executions. With the French Army in disarray, the main burden on the Western Front falls squarely upon the British.

June 7: Messines Ridge explosion

A huge underground explosion collapses the German-held Messines Ridge south of Ypres.

June 13: London attacked

London suffers its highest civilian casualties of the war as German airplanes bomb the city, killing 158 people and wounding 425.

July–Nov: 3rd Battle of Ypres

Known also as the Battle of Passchendaele, a series of attacks and counterattacks in rain and mud ended in the Allies advancing only five miles ("World War I battles", 2021). They claim this as a victory.

Oct 24: The Isonzo battles ended at Caporetta
Nov 7: October Revolution

The Bolsheviks, led by Vladimir Lenin and Leon Trotsky, overthrow the Russian government in the October Revolution. Lenin announces that Soviet Russia will immediately end its involvement in the war and renounces all treaties with the Allies.

Nov–Dec: Battle of Cambrai

First large-scale tank assault led by the British.

Dec 9: Britain captures Jerusalem

This ends four centuries of control by the Ottoman Empire.

1918

Feb 18: Operation Faustschlag

Also known as the Eleven Days' War, this is the last major offensive on the Eastern Front. The Central Powers capture huge territories in Estonia, Latvia, Belarus, and Ukraine, forcing the Bolshevik government of Russia to sign the Treaty of Brest-Litovsk.

March 3: Russia pulled out of the war

March–April: 2nd Battle of the Somme

Knowing the Russians are now out of the war, the Germans attack with gas and artillery, pushing the British back. But the assault runs out of steam and the Allies put a stop to the advance.

March 21: Ludendorff Offensive

An attempt to seize the advantage before US troops enter the war, the Germans push hard along the Western Front. Although successful, the land seized is not strategic, and their troops are tired.

July 15–18: 2nd Battle of the Marne

In their last main offensive, the Germans attack the Allies but are tricked by false trenches. By the time they reach the real front-line, they are outgunned by French and US troops and forced to retreat.

Aug 8–11: Battle of Amiens

The Hundred Days Offensive was one of the Allies' most successful advances and a "black day for the German Army" ("World War I battles", 2021). With a combined artillery, tank, and plane assault, the Germans collapsed.

Sept–Nov: Battles of the Meuse-Argonne

one million US soldiers take part in battles in the Argonne

Forest, and although losing many lives, they force Germany into retreat.

Sept 28: Kaiser agrees to armistice

Confronted by the strength of the Allies and defeat on the Western Front, Ludendorff and von Hindenburg urge the Kaiser to end the war and ask for an armistice.

Sept–Nov: Armistices were signed by the Central Powers

Austria-Hungary signs an armistice with Italy on November 3, leaving Germany alone in the war.

Germany signs the Armistice on November 11, officially ending World War 1—victory for the Allies and a defeat for Germany. Fighting continues until 11 a.m., with 2,738 men dying on the last day of the war.

1919

June 28: Treaty of Versailles signed

The treaty is signed exactly five years after the death of Archduke Franz Ferdinand.

7

MAJOR EVENTS & BATTLES - 1914

War was brewing long before the archduke was shot, and the assassination was just an excuse to jump into action. Austria-Hungary was the first to declare war on Serbia, which forced Germany to back them and declare war on their own enemies, Russia and France. All of them thought it would be a short war, over soon with decisive outcomes. They were not ready for other nations to join in and for the trench warfare that followed.

Germany had the Schlieffen Plan. Named after a general, it was a strategy based on one of Hannibal's victories against Rome in 216 B.C.E where he defeated a much larger opponent by turning each of the Roman flanks and destroying them (Limbach, 2016). With two enemies on either side, Germany would attack and conquer France while they held Russia in check until they could swing their entire force and wage full-scale war on them. The idea was to use a massive force in one movement to bring a quick victory.

In reality, the war began on three fronts: Germany invading Belgium and pushing toward France, Austria-Hungary attacking

Serbia, and the Russians mounting their own advance against the Germans. By the end of 1914, there were clear lines dug along the Western and Eastern Fronts.

SIEGE OF LIEGE

The fastest way for the Germans to get to Paris was to go straight across Belgium. They knew it might trigger another stand-off with Britain who had sworn to defend the smaller nation, but they decided that the risk was acceptable. At first, they demanded their army be given free passage through the country, but King Albert I refused. With a far superior number of soldiers, the Germans thought it would be over quickly but were not prepared for the resistance they met. In the end, the battle slowed the Germans enough to give the Allies time to form their own armies to defend Paris.

August 5–16

The town of Liege was critical because it was on the way to Paris, and was connected by rail which would become useful for transporting troops. However, it was also known as one of the most fortified cities in Europe at the time. With 12 modern forts surrounding it, General Otto von Emmich knew the Germans needed to overcome these obstacles quickly in order to take the village (Rickard, 2001). He gave them two days in which to carry out this plan, but they were not prepared for the resistance of the much smaller Belgian force.

On the first day, they found all the bridges had been blown, restricting their access. Instead of a weak, demoralized army, the Germans found they were up against more than they had expected. Once a demand to surrender had been refused by the Belgians the next day, the Germans began bombarding Liege, only to end up with far more casualties than anticipated. Erich von Ludendorff arrived, took over the 14th Brigade, and broke through on the east of the city, but could not advance without securing the forts.

Once again, the Belgians refused to give up and held off any further attacks. On August 7th, Ludendorff stormed the Citadel of Liege, easily taking it and giving him control of the city and two of the forts, and it was only by bringing in a Krupp 420 mm Howitzer that they were able to smash the rest of them over the following days (Rickard, 2001). The final two forts surrendered on the 16th and the Belgian army retreated.

GERMANY LOSES COLONIES

It was not only Europe that saw resistance to aggression—other Allied countries took up arms to overthrow German colonies. Togoland fell easily to British and French forces, while Cameroon put up more resistance until February 1916. South African troops attacked German South West Africa (Namibia), only managing to beat the Germans in July 1915.

Jiaozhou (Kiaochow) Bay on the Chinese coast was under German control until the Japanese took over; they then set their sights on the port of Tsingtao, which they finally captured on November 7, 1914. Meanwhile, New Zealand troops, with support from Allied ships, walked into Western Samoa (Samoa) without a casualty, and the Australians wrestled New Guinea from the Germans after a few weeks.

German East Africa (Rwanda, Burundi, and Tanzania) was different, and the loyal forces there put up a fierce fight against Indian, British, and colonial troops. The fighting raged on with large-scale assaults, and it was only on November 25, 1918, that it was all over with German commander Paul von Lettow-Vorbeck surrendering (Royde-Smith & Showalter, 2018). Although he lost, he had achieved his goal of drawing a huge number of almost 400,000 Allied soldiers away from the Western Front.

SERBIAN CAMPAIGN

Austria-Hungary wanted Serbia. It was one of the main reasons the war started in the first place. They had annexed Bosnia and Herzegovina, which angered the Serbs, and caused a number of rebellious factions to rise up, like the one that was behind the assassination of Franz Ferdinand. So, it was not a surprise when Austria-Hungary's focus was on taking the smaller country.

August 15–24

After bombarding the capital city of Belgrade with artillery, the Austrians invaded with a much smaller army of 200,000, but far better equipped. The Serbs were still regrouping after the Balkan Wars, and some of the soldiers did not even have boots on their feet! However, under the Serbian commander, Radomir Putnik, they managed to withstand a fierce four-day assault at Cer Mountain, ending on August 20th (Royde-Smith & Showalter, 2018). The Austrians withdrew to try another assault at Šabac the next day, but the outcome was the same, and after another four days, the Serbians remained unbroken adespite having lost 40,000 men.

September 7–October 4

The second offensive by the Austrians happened at the Drina River. After crossing at night, they met with Serbian resistance which stalled their attack long enough to bring in reinforcements from the north. Instead of a quick fight, it became the first trench battle of WW1 as soldiers dug themselves in for the next few weeks. Low on artillery and ammunition, there was little response from the Serbs as the Austrians continued a daily pounding of the surrounding hills.

November 16–December 15

After capturing the city of Valjevo, the Austrians pushed on to Belgrade for their third invasion. With heavy rain and snow, both sides fought hard. After initially pushing their opponents back, it was the Serbs under Radomir Putnik who found they were slowly retreating with every attack. By November 25th, the Austrians had reached the Kolubara River. It was there that a surprise counterattack by Putnik's men sent the enemy into disarray, forcing them back.

The victory came at a price as the Serbs were too stretched out, and without any way to defend their capital, they decided to leave it open to be taken. The Austro-Hungarian forces marched into Belgrade. On December 3rd, Putnik led another surprise attack that caught the celebrating enemy off-guard, pushing them past the Kolubara River and back across the border over the next few days. 170,000 Serbs were either killed, captured, or injured in the month's fighting ("Battle of Kolubara", 2020). Although it was a victory, it was only a matter of time before the Central Powers gathered to send another larger army to finish what the Austrians had started.

BATTLE OF THE FRONTIERS

A series of five attacks were planned along the frontline towns in northeastern France and Belgium. With Germany effectively pushing back the Belgian army, it concentrated on getting to Paris as quickly as possible as part of the Schlieffen Plan before turning toward Russia. France's alternative goal, Plan XVII, was to recapture the old territory it had lost in previous wars.

JAMES BURROWS

August 7–26

The French first focused on trying to retake the cities of Mulhouse and Lorraine as part of their war plan, and in both battles, they were successful in securing their objectives. But their celebrations were short-lived as the Germans reappeared, driving the French back out again.

The third assault saw the French and German forces literally bumping into each other in the dense fog of the Ardennes Forest. What began as a few skirmishes on August 21st, turned into a slaughter as the Germans opened fire with their machine guns at the colorfully-dressed French charging at them. Although casualties were high on both sides, the Germans were happy to settle into a trench war, sending their opponents into retreat.

The final two battles saw the Germans initiate the attacks. The first was at Charleroi, which saw heavy but confused fighting as both sides engaged. However, the French were outnumbered and forced to retreat. The last took place at Mons, where the British Expeditionary Force (BEF) had finally arrived as reinforcements. Acting on instinct, the commanding officer of the BEF, John French, sent his troops of 75,000 against a German force double that amount on August 23 ("World War I battles", 2021). They were vastly outnumbered and had to retreat losing 1,600 men to the Germans' 5,000 ("World War I battles", 2021).

The string of defeats was a wake-up call for the Allies.

BATTLE OF TANNENBERG

Tanneneberg was significant because there was a battle that had been fought there 500 years before during the Teutonic Wars, with the Germans being on the losing side (Beck, 2017b). They were keen to reverse history, but according to the Schlieffen Plan, they were to wait and concentrate on France first before advancing into Russia.

It was the Russians who decided to launch the first attack against the growing number of German soldiers and artillery that had begun mobilizing along the border. With a far greater number of men, the Russians had the upper hand, but everything changed after the Germans found a leak in enemy communications.

August 26–30

With a two-pronged strategy to encircle the enemy, the Russians led a successful initial assault with their First and Second Armies. After some confusion, and a withdrawal by the Germans, Paul von Hindenburg and von Ludendorff were called to take over what was beginning to look like a defeat. With their reorganizing of the army, using trains to bring in troops and provisions, they began to focus on deploying a more organized offensive.

After intercepting uncoded radio messages between the Russian commanders, the Germans realized that they could gain an advantage. The First and Second Armies had been pushed too far apart to help each other. Focusing all their energy on the Second Army, the Germans surprised the Russians on August 26th, sending them into a retreat two days later. Some soldiers threw down their weapons and ran, but they were trapped! The Russian commander, Samsonov, committed suicide once he realized he had failed.

No one is exactly sure of the number of casualties, but it is estimated that the Russian count was between 120,000 and 170,000 (at least 50,000 of those being killed) compared to the German's 13,000 casualties (Beck, 2017b). It was an incredible defeat for the much larger Russian army, while both von Hindenburg and von Ludendorff were German heroes. Although the fighting was closer to another city (what is now Olsztyn in Poland), it was named the Battle of Tannenberg as revenge for their loss 500 years before.

FIRST BATTLE OF THE MARNE

A crucial victory for the Allies who had been on the run in almost every meeting with the Germans up until that point. By stopping the German forces from advancing any further, they saved France from falling into the enemy's hands. The result of this battle was the beginning of real trench warfare across what would be called the Western Front.

September 6–12

Following the Schlieffen Plan, the Germans pushed hard toward their goal of reaching Paris. The Allies were exhausted from having to fight and retreat, and a victory for their opponents seemed likely. Paris prepared for a siege as it looked as though the city would soon be surrounded. But Joseph Joffre, the French commander, launched a counterattack on September 6th along with the BEF under John French (Duffy, 2009b).

As the Germans turned to meet the assault, they opened a 30-mile wide gap between their two units, which the BEF poured through. Although the Allies had the element of surprise, they were still on the back foot, and it was only the following day, once 6,000 reinforcements arrived by 600 taxis and buses from Paris, that the momentum was held (Duffy, 2009b). The following evening, another surprise attack split the gap open even wider, and by September 9th, the Germans had begun retreating. Once they reached the River Aisne, they stopped and dug trenches for the long haul.

Out of a total of two million soldiers fighting in the battle, the French casualties were high at 250,000, with the Germans around the same amount, and the British count at 12,733 (Duffy, 2009b). The Schlieffen Plan of fighting only one war on one front at a time had failed—the Germans were now fighting on both the Eastern and Western Fronts.

AMAZING FACT

- *Reconnaissance planes were used for the first time at Marne by the Allies to spot military positions from the air and use that information to help win the battle on the ground ("World War I: First Battle of the Marne", 2023).*

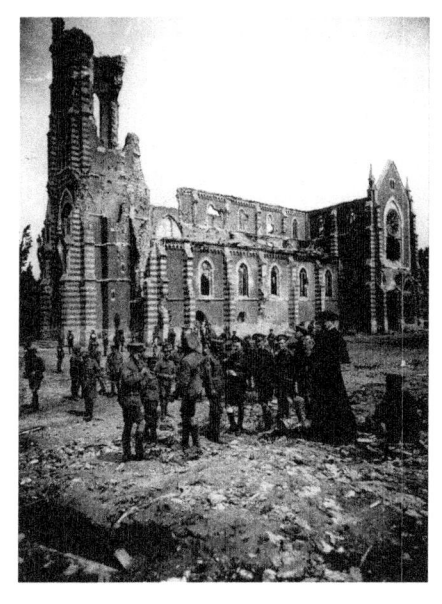

Church in Laventie, France, wrecked by German bombs

FIRST BATTLE OF YPRES

Once each side began to settle in for a trench war, the only way to crush the enemy was to outflank them—to go around their army on the sides. This became known as the "Race to the Sea." The Allies and Germans both pushed to be the first to reach a point where they could beat the other by flanking them before they got to the sea. The last strategic place this was possible to do was Ypres, a small city on the coast of Belgium.

October 19–November 22

The BEF reached Ypres, and Field Marshall John French decided that a coordinated attack with his French counterpart, Ferdinand Foch, would work. Before they could act on it, the German army chief of staff, Falkenhayn, launched an offensive on October 20th that threatened to break through the Belgian defenses. On October 27th, King Albert I of Belgium ordered the sluice gates holding back the North Sea to be opened, flooding a twenty-mile strip of land which put a halt to the German plans (McEvoy, 2009).

Falkenheyn then turned his attention to attacking the city of Ypres itself with a cavalry charge. But the British were so fast and accurate at using rifles that the Germans thought they were using machine guns and were driven back (McEvoy, 2009). Another attack was launched on November 11th, but the Germans were slow at taking advantage and a British unit made up of cooks, officer's servants, medical orderlies, clerks, and engineers finally forced them to retreat.

The fighting became intense and confusing, leaving 150,000 Allied and 130,000 German casualties, and no one gaining any territory. Only the harsh cold winter could bring the battle to an end. Private Donald Fraser said that *"one was not a soldier unless he had served on the Ypres front"* (McEvoy, 2009, para. 13).

CHRISTMAS TRUCE

December 24–25

Across the Western Front, some soldiers called an unofficial truce—a break in the war—so they could celebrate Christmas. Some carried on fighting along the trench lines, while others came out, met their enemies, exchanged gifts, sang carols, and even played friendly soccer games in no-man's-land (the area between the trenches).

One German soldier's diary said:

The English brought a soccer ball from the trenches, and pretty soon a lively game ensued. How marvelously wonderful, yet how strange it was. The English officers felt the same way about it. Thus Christmas, the celebration of Love, managed to bring mortal enemies together as friends for a time (Rees, 2009, para. 44).

Another British officer wrote:

At 8.30 I fired three shots in the air and put up a flag with "Merry Christmas" on it, and I climbed on the parapet. The Germans put up a sheet with "Thank you" on it, and the German captain appeared on the parapet. We both bowed and saluted and got down into our respective trenches, and he fired two shots in the air, and the War was on again (Rees, 2009, para. 47).

All British soldiers received packages from Princess Mary, King George V's daughter. In the metal boxes were chocolates and butterscotch, cigarettes and tobacco, a picture of Mary, and a greeting from the king.

In the midst of the insanity of war, it was a moment of human goodwill and mutual respect regardless of language or nationality.

8

MAJOR EVENTS & BATTLES - 1915

The trench war had truly begun, and it soon became clear that it would not be an easy war to win with both sides hiding behind their defenses. Many different tactics were used from gas attacks to the "creeping barrage," but neither the Allies nor Germans managed to gain real territory in any of the battles along the Western Front. The number of casualties continued to rise with very little to show for it.

In other regions, the Germans racked up a number of significant breakthroughs which strengthened the belief that the Central Powers could win the war. They held off their opponents and suffered a few defeats. The Allies, however, achieved few victories, and the British were even forced to make changes to their government to try and find a new direction.

GALLIPOLI

Meant to be a swift victory, this became one of the most disastrous Allied efforts of the entire war. With the Western Front not showing any signs of shifting, those in charge began looking for other areas where they could make an impact and change the course of the war by knocking out one of the Central Powers.

The Dardanelles provided an option both on land and at sea. It was a strait that links the Mediterranean and Black seas, and was the access point to Constantinople, the capital of the Ottoman Empire; it was a strategic point. Winston Churchill's bold idea to break through with the navy was a failure because the ships could not get through the narrow strait filled with mines and they were sitting ducks. A decision was made to forget the sea invasion and try on land.

February 17, 1915–January 9, 1916

The Gallipoli Peninsula guarded the Dardanelles Strait, and so whoever controlled this would control the sea. With a mixture of British, French, Irish, Indian, Australian, and New Zealand troops under the command of Lieutenant-General Ian Hamilton, the Allies had a total of 489,000 men to the Ottomans' 315,000 (Hickman, 2018b).

General Otto Liman von Sanders was the German commander overseeing the Turkish army, and they had already spent six weeks preparing for an assault. With no element of surprise, the Allies made two landings at Cape Helles and at Gaba Tepe. The first one on April 25th was badly managed, resulting in heavy losses, although they finally overcame the defenders. The second by the ANZACs (Australian and New Zealand troops) came off slightly better.

By April 28th, the progress had stalled, and trench warfare set in—the exact thing the Allies were trying to avoid with a swift victory! Conditions became unbearable as the heat made fighting difficult, food became inedible, and black flies swarmed over the corpses. After numerous attempts to break the deadlock in other places, all of which failed, a new Allied commander stepped in to replace Hamilton and immediately called for an evacuation.

After almost a year with nothing to show for it, Gallipoli was a complete failure. The outcome was that the Allies had 187,959 casualties and the Turks 161,828, Churchill was demoted, and the British government, under Herbert Asquith, was blamed (Hickman, 2018b).

AMAZING FACT

- *Australia and New Zealand still celebrate ANZAC day every year on April 25th, the anniversary of their beach landings at "Anzac Cove" (Hickman, 2018b).*

Anzac Day parade in London, 1919

SECOND BATTLE OF YPRES

The Allies had formed a wide defending space around the city which became known as the Ypres Salient, although the German trenches were on higher ground overlooking the British in the wet lowlands. After failing to break through the year before, another attempt by the Germans to take control of this strategic region saw renewed fighting for Ypres.

April 22–May 25

Falkenhayn wanted to attack to distract the Allies from noticing the German troop movements in the east. As part of this diversion, he ordered the use of chlorine gas. 5,000 canisters were moved near Gravenstafel Ridge where French units were stationed. With the wind behind them, they released the gas at 5 a.m. on April 22nd with devastating effects.

The unsuspecting French were immediately caught in a grey-green cloud that filled the trenches, forcing the soldiers out in the open, choking. Within an hour, 6,000 had died (Hickman, 2019b). A brutal fight followed as the Allies rushed in to close the gap. Another gas attack was released two days later, and Canadian soldiers tried using handkerchiefs soaked in urine to cover their faces for protection, but they were still pushed back.

The Germans used this tactic again, but the Allies were more prepared and, although they lost some of the higher ground, kept control of Ypres. After intense fighting, the Allies suffered 70,000 casualties, double that of the Germans (Hickman, 2019b).

AMAZING FACT

- *Canadian officer, John McRae, who was at this battle near Flanders, wrote one of the most well-known war poems for his friend who died there. Here is an excerpt:*

> *In Flanders fields the poppies blow*
> *Between the crosses, row on row,*
> *That mark our place; and in the sky*
> *The larks, still bravely singing, fly*

Scarce heard amid the guns below.

*We are the Dead. Short days ago
We lived, felt dawn, saw sunset glow,
Loved and were loved, and now we lie,
In Flanders fields.* (McRae, 1915)

WW1 produced other notable poets, including Wilfred Owens, who wrote the line, "it is sweet and fitting to die for one's country" (Owen, 1920, para. 4). Siegfried Sassoon wrote over 100 anti-war poems, vividly describing the horrors of what he had seen. He was recognized for his bravery on the battlefield and nicknamed "Mad Jack" for his courage.

GORLICE-TARNOW OFFENSIVE

This was the first time Austria-Hungary and Germany combined forces in the war and it was an extremely successful partnership. Not only did they win a surprising and quick victory, but they manage to deal a death blow to the Russian army. This went completely against the Schlieffen Plan which predicted France collapsing in a short time and a long, drawn-out war with the Russians. It was the total opposite picture in 1915.

May 2–July 13

The assault began with a massive bombardment of artillery and 40,000 soldiers against the Russians near Poland, which allowed the Central Powers to advance 10 kilometers by the first day (Lein, 2018). Although Russian reinforcements were brought to the front, they could not hold back the troops. Within eight days, the 3rd Army had collapsed, and the Russian command ordered their retreat. 100,000 Russians had been killed or wounded, and 250,000 captured (Lein, 2018).

The Central Powers had a stunning success on the Eastern Front, but for some reason, they did not repeat this winning formula of combining armies again throughout the war.

BATTLE OF LOOS

After huge defeats, the Allies were looking for a win. Joseph Joffre, the French commander, wanted to have another crack at Artois, a region he had already tried twice to take back from the Germans and failed. His was a two-pronged attack—while the French marched off to Souchez, he ordered the British to try and capture Loos. It would be another black mark on the Allies' sheet as they came up against the Germans' superior defensive strategies.

September 25–October 8

John French, the British commander ordered General Douglas Haig to carry out the attack, but Haig had serious doubts about the lack of heavy guns and shells, as well as the very open terrain they were about to attempt to march into. But the French would hear none of it.

On the first day, the British attempted their own chlorine gas attack, but the cloud did not drift all the way into enemy lines, and they ended up with 2,632 of their own casualties from it (Hickman, 2019a). Despite this setback, they managed to secure the village of Loos but ran into delays waiting for reinforcements, so had to wait. Meanwhile, the Germans reinforced their defenses.

Town of Lille completely destroyed

In the four days before the attack, the British fired over 250,00 shells at the German trenches, hoping to weaken the enemy defenses before the charge, but instead of bombarding them, it only served as a warning for the Germans to be ready for an Allied attack. On September 26th, the British marched forward in 10 assault columns without any artillery cover. In only a few minutes, they lost half of their men as the Germans opened up machine gunfire on the approaching lines. Somehow the shooting was halted as it became clear that it was just turning into a bloodbath, and the Germans allowed any survivors to retreat.

The fighting continued and an unsuccessful German counterattack to retake Loos was attempted over the following days. The British launched another failure of a gas attack, and by then any more major assaults were called off. The British had hardly made any ground for the cost of 50,000 casualties in comparison to only half that for the Germans (Hickman, 2019a). The failure was one of the main reasons John French was replaced by General Haig as the British commander.

JAMES BURROWS

SIEGE OF KUT

To end a dismal year for the Allies, all further attempts by the French against German strongholds around Champagne had failed, and there were hardly any achievements to show for all the soldiers killed and wounded. The British were also licking their wounds after being hit hard by the enemy.

Another sore point was that the Ottomans had not been easily knocked out of the war as was hoped. Focused mainly on the Western Front, British forces were spread thin across Iraq, trying to put down any opposition and a Muslim uprising. This siege was just another slap in the face for the Allies.

Machine Gun Corps. Gaza Line

December 3–April 29, 1916

Major General Charles Townshend was in charge of the Indian Expeditionary Force (IEF), a mix of British and Indian soldiers, which had unsuccessfully tried to take Baghdad from the Ottomans. On November 25th, he withdrew his 15,000 men 100 miles to a city called Kut al-Amara (Çetinsaya, 2017). The

Ottomans surrounded and tried to take Kut a few times, but after failing, set up a siege.

Inexperienced reinforcements arrived and tried four times to free the troops trapped inside but were beaten back on each attempt with over 23,000 casualties (Çetinsaya, 2017). Submarines and planes tried to send in aid, but this did not work either, and the men inside grew weaker as food ran out. After 147 days, Townshend began negotiations, even bribing the Ottoman commander, Halil, first with one and then two million pounds. When this was refused, he surrendered and was taken prisoner along with the IEF. 70% of the men died marching on foot to prison camps or while in captivity (Çetinsaya, 2017).

Although it had no great effect on the outcome of the war or the British Empire's standings in the world, it was still one of its biggest defeats. Halil said it was a Turkish victory *"the likes of which hadn't been seen for 200 years"* (Çetinsaya, 2017, para. 15).

9

MAJOR EVENTS & BATTLES - 1916

Into its third year, WW1 still showed no signs of any clear winner or loser. Both sides had suffered losses, but neither one had made any real breakthroughs that had swung the war in their favor. For all the lives lost, there was not much to show for it, and commanders were itching to prove a point. Very little territory had been won or lost.

The Allies planned a major summer attack along the River Somme in France, while the Germans had their own intentions to draw its enemies into a massive assault at Verdun. These would be the two longest and bloodiest battles of the entire war. The Russians also had been forming new plans to retaliate against the Germans, and the Italians were drawing out their skirmishes along the Isonzo against Austria-Hungary. What was supposed to be a short war entered another grueling year of attrition.

BATTLE OF VERDUN

Lasting almost a year, the cost of lives in this battle is unmatched in WW1. Designed to be a battle of attrition, the Germans wanted to hit the French so hard and so long that the number of casualties would bring them to their knees, begging for a truce. They succeeded in the first part by killing as many of their opponents as possible and wearing them out. But they failed to weaken the French who finally drove the Germans back to where they called a stop to the battle.

February 21–December 18

Located on the River Meuse, the fortress town of Verdun protected the plains of Champagne and a route into Paris. It was the perfect site for German Commander Erich von Falkenhayn's battle, and his men spent seven weeks preparing. He had to delay the start of it due to poor weather, which gave the French just enough time to move into position.

On the first morning, the Germans began with a 10-hour bombardment. Using stormtroopers who were equipped with grenades and machine guns, as well as soldiers with flamethrowers, they pushed their opponents back three miles and overran their defensive lines. General Philippe Petain took control of the French army, reinforcing the city's protection, and bringing his men to slow any further advance.

At the nearby village of Douaumont, the Germans were exposed and came under heavy fire, forcing them to abandon any further plan for a frontal assault. A change in tactic saw them target the sides of the city, and although they were successful, they were pushed back by fierce resistance each time. The Germans resorted to around-the-clock bombing of Fort Vaux and managed to take it.

The French, desperate for a break from the German advance, asked the British to start their offensive at the Somme earlier. This strategy worked as troops were suddenly withdrawn from around Verdun to meet the new threat. The Russians had also begun a new assault on the Eastern Front, and Germany scrambled to send men to help there too. With the battle stalled, Falkenhayn was replaced in August by Field Marshal Paul von Hindenburg.

In October, General Robert Nivelle of the French division began attacking the Germans near the city with heavy artillery. By November, both Fort Vaux and Douaumont were back in French hands. It cost the Germans over 430,000 men, killed or wounded, and the French lost an estimated 500,000 (Hickman, 2018a).

With so many soldiers out of action, a final joint assault was no longer possible, and Britain had to lead the "Big Push" at the end. Although it was a victory, the French would not forget the battle when they later forced a harsh Treaty of Versailles on their enemy as payback.

AMAZING FACTS

- *Because many of the soldiers were buried by the blasts or could not be identified as a result, their remains were placed in the Douaumont Ossuary, a memorial that holds 130,000 French and German soldiers' bones (Andrews, 2019).*
- *French and German armies fired between 40 and 60 million artillery shells. About 10 million unexploded shells are still in the soil around Verdun, and bomb squads are still removing 40 tons each year (admin, 2022).*
- *Nine villages near Verdun were completely destroyed during the battle, and have never been rebuilt (admin, 2022).*

BATTLE OF JUTLAND

Although the Germans and British had been in a race to see who could build the biggest navies before the war, there were not as many battles between them on the seas as there were on the

Western Front. Jutland was the only showdown between their battleships.

May 31–June 1

In order to break the Allied blockade, German Vice Admiral Reinhard Scheer decided to try and trap half the Royal Navy fleet and then battle it out with the rest later. He planned to lure Vice Admiral David Beatty's Battlecruiser Fleet to where his High Seas Fleet would be waiting and take them on. But codebreakers intercepted the plans and instead, the British sent both Beatty and Admiral John Jellicoe to meet the Germans.

When they finally encountered each other off the coast of Denmark, both sides made confusing decisions and missed opportunities resulting in a frenzied battle. The Germans scored the first points when they hit Beatty's main ship, HMS *Lion*, and sank HMS *Indefatigable* and HMS *Queen Mary*. Although Beatty got off some shots, none of them were fatal enough to sink an enemy ship, and he ended up retreating until Jellicoe arrived.

Intense fighting began the moment the entire Royal Navy Fleet was together against the High Seas Fleet. As ships engaged, a number of them took damaging hits, leaving some out of action, while others limped to get out of range of being sunk. When Jellicoe went after Scheer, the German was forced to lay a smoke screen and retreat, realizing he did not have the firepower to match his opponent. As night fell, chaotic fighting broke out as the British tried to block Scheer from getting away. But through clever maneuvers and a lack of efficient communication with the British, he managed to slip through, and by the time dawn broke, he was too far away to pursue.

250 ships and 100,000 men took part in the battle, with the British losing 14 ships to the Germans" 11 ("World War I battles", 2021). Although the Germans avoided complete destruc-

tion they never again seriously challenged British control of the North Sea.

BRUSILOV OFFENSIVE

The Russians had not yet proved themselves in the war, suffering from a number of defeats on the Eastern Front. They outnumbered the enemy by far but made too many errors and were not as well organized. They needed a win, and Aleksei Brusilov had the strategy to achieve that for them. It was so effective that it resulted in Austria-Hungary taking a backseat for the rest of the war, not being able to be involved in any major incursions.

June 4–August 10

Taking place in Galicia (modern-day northwestern Ukraine), the offensive was designed to inflict a swift, shocking attack that had been properly prepared. Brusilov had trained his men in large-scale replicas, and when they finally met the Austrians in battle on June 4th, the enemy was surprised at the power and accuracy of the Russians. Using 2,000 guns to bombard a 200-mile-long front, Brusilov's soldiers crushed the opposition, taking 26,000 prisoners in one day (Swift, 2019). Within two days, they had advanced a staggering 75 kilometers, more than any other army in the war.

The Germans were called in to help the Austrians from losing their entire army. This weakened the defenses at Verdun, helping the French finally take the upper hand there. On the Eastern Front, the Russians were not able to maintain the pressure that had hit the Austrians and finally lost steam.

The damage to the Austro-Hungarian army was irreparable and they ceased to be a major force in the war. In total, they lost between 1,000,000–1,500,000 dead, wounded, or captured to the Russians' 500,000–1,000,000 (Swift, 2019).

BATTLE OF THE SOMME

The fighting at the Somme River was one of the deadliest battles in modern history. It was another battle of attrition planned by the British with extensive bombings and attacks to inflict as much damage as possible on the enemy. The commanders always expected there to be many deaths on both sides, but this was acceptable to them as long as they did not lose more than the opposition. Very little territory was gained to justify the number of soldiers. Although it was successful for the Allies in managing to break the spirit and might of the German army, it is also seen by many as an unnecessary waste of lives.

July 1–November 13

General Douglas Haig's plans were very ambitious, and the officers struggled to meet the deadlines to have the men prepared in time, especially when the start date was brought forward to help draw Germans away from Verdun. It was all part of the "Big Push," a strategy to synchronize the Russian, French, Italian, and British offensives that would bring about the end of the war.

A week before the battle, heavy guns opened up on the German positions near the Somme. The aim was to cut through the defenses and allow free passage for the soldiers. A total of 1.5 million shells were fired but had little impact with almost 30% of them not detonating, and the rest missing targets or not having much effect on the concrete bunkers that had been built (Philpott, 2014).

On July 1, 1914, divisions rushed across ready to engage the enemy, but found much of the barbed wire and other defenses still intact! The Germans came out of their dugouts and opened fire, killing 19,000 and wounding 38,000 more (Philpott, 2014). It was a slaughter! Lieutenant Alfred Bundy ("Battle of the Somme", 2019) recorded his experience on July 1, 1916:

Suddenly... an appalling rifle and machine gun fire opened against us and my men commenced to fall. I shouted "down" but most of those that were still not hit had already taken cover. I dropped in a shell hole and occasionally attempted to move to my right and left but bullets were forming an impenetrable barrage and exposure of the head meant certain death. None of our men was visible but in all directions came pitiful groans and cries of pain' (para. 15).

WW1 Trench

Over the next few days, more attacks occurred, each one better coordinated and carried out than the last; the officers were learning from their mistakes. The Allies captured Longueval Ridge after a surprise attack on July 14th. But the breakthrough they were hoping for did not come, and a deadlock followed. In all, there were 12 separate battles with the Germans counter-attacking each time.

By September, with the fighting still carrying on across the frontline, the British introduced 32 Mark I tanks. At first, they had a shock effect on the enemy, but they were slow and difficult to maneuver and became easy targets for the Germans. After the autumn rains, everything slowed down as the terrain turned to mud, and the offensive lost its momentum and ended.

This anti-climax summed up the fighting around the Somme, and many wondered if it had been worth it. General Haig was even nicknamed "Butcher of Somme" for his role in the whole conflict. The massive count of casualties in the end was 420,000 British, 200,000 French, and around 450,000 Germans ("Battle of the Somme", 2019).

AMAZING FACTS

- *In an effort to motivate his men, Captain Wilfred "Billie" Nevill promised a prize to the first person who kicked a football into German trenches as they advanced. Some troops came into no-man's-land with footballs and a cheer, but they were cut down minutes later ("Lesser known facts", 2023).*
- *On the first day of the battle, the British suffered horrendous casualties—over 57,470, with 19,240 killed—making it the bloodiest day in British military history ("Lesser known facts", 2023).*
- *A full-length film called "The Battle of the Somme" was seen by over 20 million people after it came out in August 1916. Instead of boosting morale, many were upset by what they saw ("Lesser known facts", 2023).*
- *Adolf Hitler injured his leg at the Somme after shrapnel from an explosive went off near him. He was also involved in the First Battle of Ypres and later at Passchendaele ("Lesser known facts", 2023).*

10

MAJOR EVENTS & BATTLES - 1917

With both sides assessing their damages after the intense battles of 1916, the key was to ensure there were enough troops to send into the Western and Eastern Fronts. The Allies were growing with reinforcements. With 3.9 million soldiers to the Germans' 2.5 million, their superiority in numbers meant they could now go on the attack. In response, the Germans, under Ludendorff and von Hindenburg, decided to pull back to their defensive lines and settle even more into a deadlock. But it was Russia struggling back at home because of the Bolshevik Revolution overthrowing Tsar Nicholas, and the United States entering the war that caused the biggest shift in the war.

VIMY RIDGE

As part of a much larger offensive planned by the new French commander, General Nivelle, this was a strategic move to gain higher ground. The seven-kilometer Vimy Ridge overlooked both Arras and Artois and securing it would put the Allies in a commanding position. The Canadian Corps was given a task that the French had already failed, losing 100,000 casualties there.

April 9–12

Weeks of training and rehearsing went into the attack, with specialized groups of machine-gunners, riflemen, and flamethrowers being formed. Deep tunnels were dug to get the men as close to the front as possible. For seven days before the assault, artillery pounded the enemy trenches, this time with accuracy and precision, destroying German defenses.

The Canadian Corps commander, Julian Byng, warned his men *"Chaps, you shall go over exactly like a railroad train, on time, or you shall be annihilated"* (Cook, 2015, para. 3). And that is exactly what happened. With 1,000 artillery guns providing supportive fire as they went, the soldiers stormed the ridge. 15,000 rushed up, continuing the offensive even when their officers were killed. They captured both the frontline and the second line within 30 minutes despite a snowstorm. Many were involved in a bayonet charge of the final machine gun nest that held the top.

The Canadians lost over 3,000 men and around 7,000 were wounded, but it was still a huge success (Cook, 2015). Despite the British not being able to win their battles, the taking of Vimy Ridge stands out as a crucial win.

AMAZING FACT

- In 1922, the French gave Canada Vimy Ridge and the land around it as a reward for the incredible sacrifice they made. A memorial stands there now as a reminder of the Canadians' courage (Cook, 2015).

MESSINES

This was another battle designed to take over the 250-foot-high ridge of Messines near Ypres. The Germans had enjoyed a commanding position by holding on to it, and it was critical that the high point be taken. Instead of relying on charging in, the plan was to blow up the enemy, and one of the biggest explosives operations was set into place.

June 7–14

For over a year, tunnels had been dug underneath German trenches, some of them extending over a mile and 300 feet deep—a difficult job to do, considering it had to be kept secret, and many lost their lives when shafts collapsed. But by June, the excavations were ready and filled with 600 tons of explosives.

At 3 a.m., the landscape changed as the biggest detonation went off, immediately killing 10,000 Germans and destroying the town as well (Routledge, 2021). At that time in history, it was the largest man-made explosion in history! By 7 a.m., using a "creeping barrage" where artillery moved slowly forward, firing every few meters as infantry marched behind them, Messines was taken by New Zealand troops.

Major General Charles Harington had been right when he said, *"Gentlemen, I do not know whether we shall change history tomorrow, but we shall certainly alter the geography"* (Routledge, 2021, para. 3).

AMAZING FACT

- *The explosion was heard 140 miles away and left a crater 145 ft deep and 380 ft wide, some of which is still visible today (Routledge, 2021).*

THIRD BATTLE OF YPRES

Also known as the Battle of Passchendaele, it was another example of what WW1 had become: a senseless, mad slaughter in the mud! General Haig's plan was to break the Germans' stronghold around Ypres once and for all, bringing an end to the deadlock in the area. After the incredible success of Messines, the British were overly optimistic choosing an "all-out" attack. But the rain caused a miserable slog, and the battle did not amount to much in the end except an enormous number of deaths.

July 31–November 6

3,000 guns shot 4.5 million shells at the enemy lines, but it was not enough to destroy the concrete pillboxes where the German machine guns were kept (Roy & Foot, 2023). The rain and explosions turned everything into a muddy wasteland, making it difficult for soldiers and tanks to attack. Instead of abandoning another attack, Haig ordered them to push on, resulting in 70,000 casualties on the British side alone.

The Canadians managed one victory by attacking the town of Lens, but other than that, the fighting stalled, and Haig came under pressure to abort. Instead of withdrawing, he pushed on when the weather improved. Using the "creeping barrage" approach, the Allies made some progress, and things began looking up. Haig believed the Germans were on the verge of collapsing and fresh attacks were ordered during October. The muddy conditions returned with the rain, and all of them failed to achieve anything.

It turned into a nightmare. Even the beautiful nature that once covered the area had been completely destroyed. As Private R.A. Colwell (Browne, 2019) said:

There was not a sign of life of any sort. Not a tree, save for a few dead stumps which looked strange in the moonlight. Not a bird, not even a rat or a blade of grass. Nature was as dead as those Canadians whose bodies remained where they had fallen the previous autumn. Death was written large everywhere (para. 18).

While trying to take the Passchendaele Ridge, soldiers huddled in water-filled shell holes against the torrential downpour and explosions. Some got lost trying to find their way back to their lines. Rifles jammed and stretcher-bearers had to wade through waist-deep mud as conditions became worse. Finally, once a few high points had been taken, Haig called an end to the attacks. Both sides suffered with 270,000 casualties on the Allied side and 220,000 on the German side (Roy & Foot, 2023).

No real objectives were gained, and another pointless battle ended with nothing other than death.

AMAZING FACT

- *In 1918, during the Spring Offensive led by the Germans, instead of trying to defend the Passchendaele Ridge, the British gave it up without firing one shot.*

BATTLE OF CAMBRAI

Cambrai was another battle that saw the British advance and take ground only to lose it again later to the Germans. However, it was different because of the methods and equipment. The first-ever full-scale tank attack using a proper tank division, it changed the way modern wars would be fought from that moment.

JAMES BURROWS

American WW1 tank

November 20–December 5

With over 400 Mark VI tanks, each with a crew of eight and able to travel at 6 km/h, the British pushed deep into enemy territory (Kennedy, 2016). It was a huge change to the very first introduction of tanks, and it showed everyone just how devastating they could be when used properly. Working alongside artillery and infantry, the move was very successful at first.

But there were still issues, and after the first day, only half of the tanks were still in operation. Many of them had mechanical issues or were targeted by enemy artillery. Doing what they were best at, the Germans quickly filled with reinforcements and secured their defenses. A counterattack saw the British lose much of the territory that had just been taken. It was this battle that gave the German officers the idea that they were still strong enough to carry out an offensive that would break the Allies before the Americans arrived.

11

MAJOR EVENTS & BATTLES - 1918 AND HOW THE WAR ENDED

With Russia finally pulling out of the war, the British expected the Germans to turn their full attention to the Western Front, especially before the United States joined in the war. Their plan was not to attack but defend along the Western Front in the hopes that they could wait long enough for the new reinforcements. The Spring Offensive was Germany's last major invasion, a desperate attempt to break the trench deadlock and beat France and Britain while they still had a chance.

Once the Americans arrived, things quickly turned against the Central Powers. Fresh soldiers and equipment filled the ranks of the Allies, who shifted from defense into offense in a series of battles that finally brought the war to an end. At this time, Woodrow Wilson, the US president, played a major role in pushing for peace.

SPRING OFFENSIVE

General Ludendorff had begun planning a series of attacks that were designed to split the British and French. Broken up into five main phases, each part focused on specific objectives that needed to work for the Germans to have any chance of facing off against the Americans. However, Ludendorff had underestimated the fighting spirit of what he thought was a weak, trench-bound opposition, and met with more resistance than expected.

Operation Michael: March 21–April 5

Sometimes called the Second Battle of the Somme, this attack began with massive artillery fire, gas, and smoke screens, with the German infantry advancing five hours later. Stormtroopers used foggy conditions in their surprise assault and the defensive line was pushed back. A number of battles followed along the line, most of them successful for Ludendorff's men, capturing 3,100 km² of territory (Watson, 2016). However, none of this land was of any real strategic value.

The other downside was that the Germans advanced so quickly, they were far from their lines and had to slow down enough for supplies to catch up. This gave the Allies enough time to bring in reinforcements and slow the advance even more. After a few days, the offensive ran out of steam and was called off. The British had held their defenses, and although it was severely bent at times, never broke.

Operation Georgette: April 9–29

This next phase was intended to capture the rail hub at Hazebrouk which would be an opening to take the port and cut off those troops guarding Ypres. Another intense attack was launched, hitting the Allies hard enough for them to collapse and withdraw. Messines and the Passchendaele Ridge were taken back, and the British were stretched to hold their line along the River Lys.

Another concentrated push would have seen Ludendorff break through to the port 15 miles away.

But he spread out his attack and lost the initiative. Added to that, there were more logistical problems slowing the Germans down, and the offensive ended without Hazebrouk as their prize.

Operation Blücher–Yorck: May 27–July 18

The focus of this part of the Spring Offensive was to draw French troops away from the coast and split the Allied forces. Once again, the initial German attack was successful, breaking the frontlines of the opposition, and opening the way through to the River Marne, 90 miles from Paris (Watson, 2016). The French government ordered an evacuation of the city in fear of it being conquered.

American troops came onto the scene at this point, recapturing Cantigy, Vaux, and Belleau Wood. This was a huge boost for the Allies who had been on the back foot for most of the German offensive. Meanwhile, Ludendorff overextended his reach again, spreading his troops thin across a large area.

Operation Gneisenau: June 9–12

The fourth phase followed the pattern of the others. The Germans made incredible progress, hoping to widen the area they held, linking with their territory at Amiens. But the French had been warned of the attack through prisoners they had captured and launched a fierce counterattack on June 11th. With no initial bombardment to warn them, the Germans were caught off guard. Facing 150 tanks and 4 French divisions, Ludendorff's objectives came to another standstill.

Second Battle of the Marne: July 15–18

Under the name of Operation Friedensturm, this was the last assault of the Germans. Ludendorff wanted to divert troops away from Flanders where he had planned to have another attack at a later date. This time, however, they had little success in the beginning as they were fooled by false trenches dug along the frontlines by the French and held back ("World War I battles", 2021). Although they managed to cross the Marne, a swift counterattack pushed the Germans back, losing much of the ground they had taken in the third phase.

It was a critical defeat signaling the end of the German offensives. From that moment on, all the momentum shifted to the Allies.

BATTLE OF AMIENS

This was the first battle in what became known as the Hundred Days Offensive. Seeing the disarray in the German forces after the Second Battle of the Marne, Marshal Ferdinand Foch proposed striking key points like the Amiens railway junction. Learning from their mistakes, the Allies began to implement better tactics which saw a more flexible infantry working alongside tanks and aircraft. The combination overwhelmed the Germans, making it one of their worst defeats.

August 8–12

Secretly, a huge force was assembled including 500 tanks, 1,900 aircraft, 2,000 artillery pieces, and a huge contingent of troops made up of French, British, American, Canadian, and Australian soldiers (Badsey, 2016). The Allies far outnumbered the Germans.

With no bombardment to announce their intentions, they

attacked with a "creeping barrage," completely taking the enemy by surprise. Using speed, the French then broke through the defensive lines, seizing critical points. It was the first time tanks and infantry worked together, and although there was some miscommunication, as a whole, it was effective. Toward the end of the battle, mechanical issues and losses had reduced the tank numbers down to only six. Aircraft also played an integral role, providing cover from the air, and keeping the Germans on the back foot during the conflict.

This time, Haig did not push the advantage. Learning from the bloodbath of previous attritional assaults, after only four days, he pulled all his men back to focus on a new fresh charge.

Ludendorff saw it as one of the worst defeats, calling it a "black day of the German Army" (Badsey, 2016, para. 4). As a result of the failure of the Spring Offensive and the demoralizing impact Amiens had, the German commanders realized they had lost the Western Front. Compared to the 44,000 casualties suffered by the Allies, the Germans had to deal with over 75,000, with 30,000 more surrendering during the battle (Badsey, 2016).

In contrast to the Battle of Frontiers four years earlier, Amiens showed just how far the Allies had progressed and transformed their tactics and technology.

BATTLE OF MEGIDDO

The Ottoman Empire had been using World War 1 and its alliance to try and regain control over the territory it had lost in the Balkan Wars. Although its army had showed fighting spirit in Gallipoli and other Mediterranean efforts, its influence in the region was limited. Having lost the city of Jerusalem to the British at the end of 1917, the battle for Palestine was their last hope of holding onto power in the Middle East. The Allies knew if they could knock them out there, they would be finished.

JAMES BURROWS

September 19–25

General Edmund Allenby had led battalions during the Boer War in South Africa and was given the task of taking Palestine from the Turks. He was not a stranger to hot, dry conditions, and adapted to the semi-desert of the Middle East very quickly. He saw the usefulness of combining technology with infantry, and this approach worked.

Instead of attacking Gaza, Allenby chose to surround the enemy and take Beersheba. After deceiving the Ottoman forces into thinking the assault would come from the east and not from the desert, they were totally unprepared for the battle. The British bombarded the enemy shortly before a daring attack by the Australian Light Horse Brigade broke the defenses and opened the way to Gaza.

Coastal guns in Middle East, 1918

From that moment the Turks were always on the back foot as they retreated further and further until they tried a counterattack at Megiddo. But Allenby had always planned for that to happen, and using a combination of air, cavalry, artillery, and infantry, they forced the trapped enemy into a no-win situation. The battered Ottoman Army surrendered having lost 25,000 men, either killed, wounded, or captured ("Battle of Megiddo", 2019a).

The rest of the region was easily taken as Allied forces moved through to Damascus. The Ottomans signed an armistice ending their role in the war, and effectively, their empire.

MEUSE-ARGONNE OFFENSIVE

The Allies planned to push the Germans out of France and back behind the Hindenburg Line, back into their own country. It was a large-scale offensive with all the major players taking part, the US bringing over one million of their own soldiers to the fight (Stewart, 2005). Because the Germans had occupied the region for so long, the defense systems were sturdy and elaborate, with barbed wire, machine-gun positions, and concrete fighting posts, and the Allies faced stiff resistance.

September 26–November 11

General Pershing, the US commander, launched his attack early on the first day with a three-hour bombardment of the enemy lines. Although the Americans quickly overran the first line, they slowed as German reinforcements came in, and the rain turned the Meuse River and Argonne Forests into a muddy war zone.

The first several weeks of October saw the fighting intensify as the Allies pushed harder, while the Germans held onto their high positions, firing down on the attackers. The Americans shifted from an all-out attack to small sporadic assaults, wearing the enemy down before another massive assault. This was a new tactic, rather than the "Big Push" the British and French had been so committed to during most of the Western Front battles.

November 1st saw the well-prepared Americans advance in full force, pushing the Germans deep behind their own lines. 43 German divisions were forced back over 30 miles of heavily fortified positions. It was a resounding success.

The victory claimed 26,000 American lives with 120,000 more wounded, making it the deadliest battle in US history ("World War I battles", 2021). Their role in the battle helped end the German defense once and for all. One week later, the Armistice was signed by Germany on Field Marshal Ferdinand Foch's personal train at the eleventh hour of the eleventh day of the eleventh month—November 11, 1918.

Wall Street celebrates on the day Germany surrendered

12

LIFE IN THE TRENCHES

The western frontlines of Europe were a series of long, narrow channels dug into the ground where soldiers could hide from enemy fire. These were the trenches of World War 1. Some of them were fortified with elaborate bunker systems, but most were just muddy, unhygienic ditches. It was not a new system, having already been used in the US Civil War and others, but it proved effective during the first half of the war as a defense for dealing with the new weaponry such as machine guns. However, it was not ideal for the men on both sides as disease, rats, and boredom were a large part of life waiting in the trenches.

MUD

The forest region of France and Belgium, where the Western Front was situated, had torrential rains in the spring and snow in the winter. These conditions were not ideal for living in trenches, which were sometimes little more than holes in the ground. In the rainy season, these dugouts would fill with water, causing major problems for the men.

JAMES BURROWS

Even though pumps were used, water and mud in the trenches was always a problem. Finding a dry place to sleep was almost impossible. Passchendaele was one of the worst as water often came up to waist-high level. This made living conditions very difficult and a disease called trench foot was common. Caused when the feet are always wet, trench foot damages nerves and circulation which brings dead tissue, resulting in incredible pain. Soaked through, soldiers had no way of keeping their feet dry and often smeared whale oil on them to protect them from getting the disease ("Why whales were vital", 2023).

STINK

Before even getting into the trenches or seeing the mud, soldiers would smell them! With so many dirty men squashed together, the stagnating mud and water, and rotting corpses on the frontline, the odor was already bad. But, it was also the fact that latrines (toilets) were dug inside the trenches for men to relieve themselves, many of them overflowing, that added to the stink. To try and neutralize the smell, chloride and lime were sprinkled across, but this often added to the stench of the trench ("Life in the trenches", 2000). Often new reinforcements that arrived would be sick from the smell.

Robert Graves (1957) in his book, *Goodbye To All That*, describes what it was like:

The smell was a compound of stagnant mud, latrine buckets, chloride of lime, unburied and half-buried corpses, rotting sandbags, stale human sweat, fumes of cordite and lyddite. Sometimes it was sweetened by cigarette smoke and the scent of bacon frying over wood fires, sometimes made sinister by the lingering odor of poison gas (p. 84).

Highland Territorials in a trench.

PESTS

It was not only soldiers in the trenches. Being surrounded by forests, rivers, and mud, the unsanitary conditions also attracted animals, some falling in, others looking for food. Robert Graves (1957) remembers there were *"Hundreds of field mice and frogs were in the trench. They had fallen in and had no way out. The light dazzled them and we could not help treading on them"* (p. 85).

But the worst pests were rats and lice. With so many dead bodies around, the rats had a feast, gorging on rotting flesh. Some of them grew to be as "as big as cats" ("Life in the trenches", 2000, para. 5). Disease spread rapidly through the dug-outs because of these vermin. The lice weren't any better. It was only after the war that doctors realized they contributed to what was called "trench fever," by giving men headaches and other sickly symptoms.

RATIONS

Food became a major problem. Trying to source enough to feed two million men was a hard job, especially on the frontlines where fresh vegetables were not always available. Sometimes, weeds, leaves, and nettles were used to flavor soup (Cadman-Rivers, 2014). Much of the bread and biscuits were stale by the time they arrived at the trenches.

Tommies eating in a trench

The other issue was cooking it in the middle of nowhere. Each battalion had two industrial-sized vats to make food in, but these could not be washed properly every time, and after a while, everything started to taste like pea-horse soup! One of the most hated by the British was a canned soup called Machonochie, which was so bad, it was only eaten by those who were starving (Cadman-Rivers, 2014). When flour became an issue throughout Europe, cooks turned to baking bread from dried potatoes, oats, barley, and sometimes crushed straw. Most soldiers drank tea to try and hide the taste of the water that had been transported in petrol cans and filtered with chemicals.

Not wanting the enemy to know they were struggling, the British were forbidden from complaining about their food to show the Germans that they were all a happy, well-fed platoon!

AMAZING FACT

- *Soup powder and custard powder, as we have in shops today, were invented during World War 1 to make cooking easier and quicker on the frontlines (Cadman-Rivers, 2014).*

ROUTINE

Unless a soldier was part of an attack, life in trenches became monotonous and boring. To try and keep the men fresh, they had a pattern of four days in the trench, four days in reserve, and then four days resting. Otherwise, the day-to-day routine was the same to keep order in the frontlines.

- **Dawn**: Soldiers would be up and ready at their firing positions in case of an enemy attack. The British would hear their commander giving the order, "Stand to!" which told every man to be at their posts (Baker, 2019).
- **Daily:** Sentries would be on watch and an officer would check in with them every hour. No one could leave their post without permission, and full uniform and gear had to be worn when on duty. Bayonets needed to be attached at night or during fog in case of attacks.

Rifle inspections would happen every day to ensure the weapons were not full of mud or sand. A gas gong was an empty shell casing that would be hit to give everyone warning of a gas attack and to put on masks.

- **Night**: This was when supplies would be brought into the frontline under cover of darkness. But the enemy knew this and often tried to target supply roads and tracks that were used.

Barracks built into the ground

Construction parties would come in and fix duckboards (raised wooden walkways), sandbags, and other equipment. Patrols would use this time to check out any enemy listening posts or weaknesses in the defenses.

The best way to get a small idea of what it was like in the trenches as a soldier is to read a bit from Rifleman William Eve's diary entry ("1915: Early trench battles", n.d.) on January 7, 1915:

Poured with rain all day and night. Water rose steadily till knee-deep when we had the order to retire to our trenches. Dropped blanket and fur coat in the water. Slipped down as getting up on parapet, got soaked up to my waist. Went sand-bag filling and then sewer guard for 2 hours. Had no dug out to sleep in… In one place we had to go through about 2 feet of water. Were sniped at a good bit... Roache shot while getting water and Tibbs shot while going to his aid. He laid in open all day, was brought in in the evening, unconscious but still alive. Passed away soon after (para. 3).

SHELL SHOCK

Not being able to cope with war was seen as a weakness and was a punishable offense. No one knew about PTSD (Post Traumatic Stress Disorder) or as it came to be known, "Shell Shock." But war had changed. The modern artillery and weapons were louder, deadlier, and more rapid than in wars before. By the end of World War 1, there were lots of soldiers with similar symptoms after being exposed to detonating shells around them or horrific bombardments and attacks.

The constant sound of war was all around as Robert Graves (1957) describes:

A German shell came over and then whoo - oo - oooooOOO - bump - CRASH!... Rifle bullets in the open went hissing into the grass without much noise, but when we were in a trench the bullets, going over the hollow, made a tremendous crack. Bullets often struck the barbed wire in front of the trenches, which turned them and sent them spinning in a head-over-heels motion - ping! rockety-ockety-ockety-ockety into the woods behind (p. 83).

Some men suffered from shaking, trembling, stammering, paralysis, and speech disorders, while others broke into tears, had nightmares, or began sleepwalking (Alexander, 2010). Doctors at the time were struggling to understand what it was and how to treat it. It is estimated that close to 80,000 cases of shell shock were officially documented (Alexander, 2010).

13

HEROIC FEATS

Kings, kaisers, tsars, and generals always end up stealing the spotlight in wars because they are the ones who make the big decisions and say the memorable speeches. But the battles would not be fought if it wasn't for ordinary soldiers running between trenches, jumping through barbed wire, and giving their lives as they face off across muddy terrain. It is these courageous individuals that help break through the defense lines and change the outcome of a conflict because of their bravery.

Although many of the main roles were filled with males, especially when it came to fighting, there were a number of women who made headlines in their own ways. They rose above the call of duty and served their countries.

There were many different medals for soldiers serving in the army and even for civilians performing military tasks. But the most recognized were those each country awarded for incredible acts of bravery:

Great Britain gave out 633 Victoria Cross medals to individuals during the war, their highest military award ("Victoria Cross", n.d.).

The US handed out 126 Medals of Honor *"for gallantry and bravery in combat at the risk of life above and beyond the call of duty"* ("World War I Medal of Honor", 2022, para. 1) and an extra 6 went to nameless soldiers of Belgium, France, Great Britain, Italy, Romania, and the United States to commemorate those who died .

The War Cross, or Croix de Guerre, was the top French medal awarded to Allied soldiers who showed courage under fire ("The War Cross", 2018).

The Germans used the Iron Cross, a symbol known for bravery during the war, painted on planes and military vehicles. It was awarded for incredible feats in battle, but toward the end, it was handed out to try and boost morale, with over 163,000 first class and 5,000,000 second class being awarded, making almost one in every third soldier a recipient! (Wernitz, 2014)

MILITARY

Sir Adrian Carton de Wiart

De Wiart served in the Boer War, World War 1, and World War 2. Against his father's consent, he enlisted to serve in South Africa even though he was underage. While he was there, he was shot in the stomach and the groin and was taken back to England where he had to wait more than 10 years to be a soldier again.

In November 1914, he was serving in the Somaliland Camel Corps when he was shot in the arm and face, losing his left eye and part of his ear (Crutchley, 2015). Not one to sit on the sidelines, he threw his glass eye out of a taxi and went straight back to the war where he ended up in the Second Battle of Ypres. Once again, he was injured when German artillery shattered his left hand. Apparently, the doctor refused to amputate the fingers, and de Wiart ended up ripping them off himself!

Amazingly, with one eye and one hand, he was allowed back into battle where he took command of the 8th Battalion at the Somme in 1916 (Crutchley, 2015). Not able to use his left hand, he ended up pulling the pins from grenades with his teeth, and then throwing them at the enemy, an act of recklessness gaining him the Victoria Cross. Here he was also shot through the back of the head, the bullet missing his spinal cord.

Later, he would also serve in WW2, swimming ashore when his plane was shot down, and attempting numerous escapes from a POW camp. Dodging death so many times, Adrian Carton de Wiart lived to the incredible age of 83 years old (Crutchley, 2015).

Instead of the grim horrors of the Western Front, he wrote in his autobiography, *"Frankly, I had enjoyed the war"* (Crutchley, 2015, para. 8).

Henry Johnson

The "Harlem Hellfighters" was an American National Guard Unit made up completely of black soldiers. Even though they did not have the same rights as others in their own country, they still chose to fight just like every soldier in the war. Their troops saw some of the toughest fighting on the Western Front.

Johnson was 25 years old and worked as a railway baggage handler when he joined the Harlem Hellfighters. He became their most famous member because of his single stand against a whole unit of enemy soldiers.

During the night of May 14, 1918, he and his partner, Needham Roberts, were on sentry watch in the trenches about 115 miles from Paris when they heard noises ("WW1 heroes", 2020). Johnson fired a flare into the sky only to see a whole platoon of Germans rushing at them. Grenades began exploding around them, the blast hitting Johnson on the left side. Roberts was also hit, but helped throw grenades back.

Johnson shot one German at point-blank range, then swung his rifle up like a club to smack another one, hitting until the weapon broke in his hands ("WW1 heroes", 2020). Grabbing his knife, he stabbed two more. Johnson was shot in the shoulder and leg, but he managed to slash and cut another opponent. Realizing they were not gaining any ground against one madman, the Germans retreated as Johnson hurled grenades after them.

Even though he had 21 wounds from the fight, he still managed to single-handedly fend off about 20 German soldiers, killing 4 of them ("WW1 heroes", 2020).

Alvin York

Alvin York never wanted to go to war. Because of his faith, he didn't think it was the right thing to do, and he tried to be exempted from being called up. His application was denied, and he was drafted into the American Army and sent to Europe to take part in the Meuse Argonne Offensive.

On October 8, 1918, his patrol was given the task of taking down a German machine-gun battalion ("Alvin York", 2023). They did not get far when they were pinned down by the intense shooting from the enemy, York's commander and a few others getting wounded in the process. With the rest of the men in defensive positions, he took control of the situation and alone began firing back.

York's skill as an expert hunter kicked in. Shooting with precision and speed, he killed more than a dozen enemy soldiers on his own. Seeing they were getting picked off one by one, some of the Germans tried to charge, but York killed them too. The German officer realized they were not going to win against such marksmanship and surrendered his unit of 90 men ("Alvin York", 2023). While York was marching his captives back, he forced them to convince other German soldiers to surrender. He reached the American lines with 132 prisoners ("Alvin York", 2023).

Edouard Izac

Izac was born in Iowa, US, but his parents originally came from Germany, so he understood the language very well. This would play a significant role later when he joined the war.

At the age of 25, he graduated from the Naval Academy and finally entered WW1 as a gunnery officer on a transport ship. After five successful trips transporting troops across to Europe, they ran into a German U-boat, and on May 31, 1918, three torpedoes hit the USS *President Lincoln,* sinking it in less than 30 minutes (Harper, 2021). Lt. Edouard Izac was taken prisoner as he was one of the highest-ranking officers left alive.

On board the U-boat, Izac moved around freely, even playing cards with the crew. Not knowing he could speak German, they all spoke openly in front of him, and Izac learned about the submarine's design, capabilities, and plans. Realizing he had enemy intelligence for his superiors, he began a series of escape attempts.

One after the other they all failed, especially the crazy stunt of jumping out of the window of a moving train. For that, he ended up badly injured from the fall and badly beaten as punishment! It was only in October, after months in POW camps, that Izac finally escaped and set off for the neutral country of Switzerland. After one week of traveling 120 miles on foot, stealing vegetables, and sneaking past German sentries, Izac and another escapee made it. Later that month, he was able to relay all the information he had gathered.

For his bravery, determination, and cunning, he was given the Medal of Honor and was 98 years old when he died in 1990, the last living recipient of this award (Harper, 2021).

John Cornwell

The youngest person to be awarded a Victoria Cross, Cornwell was only 16 years old when he was fatally injured at the Battle of Jutland.

John "Jack" Cornwell grew up in East London winning no prizes for sports or achieving great results at school. He did, however, excel in Boy Scouts where he racked up a number of badges for completing certain tasks. With his passion for scouts and having a father who had served as a soldier, it was no surprise that he ended up leaving school and enlisting with the Royal Navy at the age 15 (Hemmings, 2019).

In February 1916, he was given the rank of Boy First Class and joined the crew aboard the HMS *Chester* (Hemmings, 2019). His job was to set the sights for the ships' 5.5-inch gun, a dangerous position when being attacked. On May 31st, four German light cruisers trapped them and began firing. Cornwell's gun was hit, killing the crew and wounding him. With shrapnel in his leg and stomach, Cornwell remained standing at his post for another hour waiting for orders while the captain managed to steer the *Chester* away from the enemy.

Cornwell died two days later of his injuries and was given a hero's burial. Later, the Boy Scouts Cornwell Badge was designed and awarded to boys showing valor and bravery.

Georges Guynemer

Rejected by the military when he tried to join because of health issues, Guynemer became a mechanic for the French Air Force. After training, he became a pilot and joined the elite French squadron where he ended up flying one of the SPAD VII and later the SPAD XIII fighter planes (Hickman, 2017).

Although he ended up as a hero because of his ace flying and 53 kills, it was his conduct in the air that won him the respect of France. In 1917, he was involved in an intense dogfight with the legendary Ernst Udet, one of Germany's best pilots (Hickman, 2017). Dodging and weaving in the air, they both tried to pin the other with their cannons. It was during this battle that Udet's guns jammed, and he became a sitting duck for Guynemer.

Instead of taking his chance, Guynemer waved his hands at his enemy to show that he was not about to be unsporting. Without taking the shot, the French pilot flew off, leaving Udet to fight another day.

Guynemer's plane went down after engaging with German fighters on September 11, 1916.

Flora Sandes

Sandes was the only British woman to serve as a soldier in WW1. Different from other women, she enjoyed shooting and riding and learned to drive a car. When the war broke out, she traveled to Siberia as a nurse. By the time the Siberian Army was forced to retreat by Bulgarian forces, Sandes was serving as a soldier. Someone noticed how she rode a horse and suggested she try out as a combatant rather than a nurse. Taking her Red Cross badge off her arm, she joined as a private and became known as "Serbia's Joan of Arc" ("Flora Sandes", n.d.).

Never one to back down, Sandes served at the frontline until she was wounded by a Bulgarian grenade in 1916. During her recovery, she was awarded the Serbian Order of the Kara-George, a distinction not many others were given for their acts of bravery. By the end of the war, she had received the rank of captain.

"People do love to tell you you can't do things" she once said ("Flora Sandes", n.d., para. 5).

Maria Bochkareva

Born into a poor Russian family and with a tough upbringing, Bochkareva wrote to the tsar to allow her to enlist in the army. When she was allowed to, she joined the army, but was not always accepted by the men, and often had to fight to prove herself. Living in the trenches, eating the same rations, she was injured a few times and received a number of awards for her bravery.

In 1917, she was given command of her own unit, the 1st Battalion of Death, made up only of 300 women that Bochkareva handpicked (Goodridge, 2018). They were part of Russia's last offensive against Germany.

When Russia fell to the Bolsheviks after Tsar Nicholas II was forced off the throne, she found herself on the wrong side. She was imprisoned, interrogated, and executed as an enemy of the people.

Heine von Heimburg

Although fighting for the side that lost, there were still soldiers who bravely served their country. As a German naval officer of a submarine, von Heimburg is most well-known for his daring escape through the Dardanelles, past British ships.

Aboard the Ocarina, a German submarine U-22, the chances of getting through the Dardanelles was one in fifty (Bronner, 2023)! With strong artillery on either side and a patrol of destroyers, von Heimburg had no choice but to submerge. This created another problem because the British also had steel nets strapped across the entrance to the main waterways. These had a glass float attached to the top, so if something pushed or pulled the net below, the float would move and alert those above.

The Ocarina got caught, and von Heimburg's attempts to submerge or reverse only caused the net to snap, which alerted the destroyers. They began firing but the German submarine was too deep. Instead of retreating, von Heimburg gave the order for full speed ahead, pulling the net and the floats down beneath the surface. But the net jammed his motor and he could do nothing but wait until dark while the British tossed depth charge bombs down.

At night, the submarine surfaced with no destroyers in sight. Armed with hammers and hatchets, the crew cut the net loose and went on their way. Heine von Heimburg had gone through the Dardanelles and won the German order of bravery, *"Pour le Merité"* (Bronner, 2023).

Otto von der Linde

The youngest officer to win the *"Pour le Merité,"* Lieutenant Otto von der Linde conquered a fort without firing a shot.

As part of the Fifth Guards marching through Belgium, their path was blocked by the forts of Namur, especially Fort Malonne, a stronghold that was impenetrable. Surrounding the fort was an open plain, and it would be suicide to cross without artillery. Von der Linde spoke up, telling his senior officers he would take the fort with only four men. It was crazy, but they decided to let him try.

Marching out across the plain, the men arrived at the gate of the fort while the Belgian commander looked down. Von der Linde lied that the forests were filled with artillery ready to bomb the fort if the men did not surrender. The gate opened and 25 men gave up their weapons while another 300 escaped out the back.

Pulling down the Belgian flag, von der Linde made a German flag using black pants, a white shirt, and a red undershirt. When a general later came riding past and asked who was in command, von der Linde proudly introduced himself and his army of four!

Sergeant Stubby

Animals were not uncommon in WW1 as horses, mules, pigeons, and dogs played vital roles in communication and transport. But very few received awards for their brave deeds, and hardly any got as many as Sergeant Stubby, a pit bull dog.

As part of the 102nd Infantry, 26th Yankee Division, Stubby belonged to Private Conroy and served in 17 battles (Walker, 2020). After being injured by a mustard gas attack, he became very good at detecting when the Germans released this gas on the frontlines. With incredible hearing, Stubby could also alert the soldiers to incoming artillery since his ears could pick up the faint whine long before humans. He also provided comfort to injured men in no-man's-land while they waited for medical help.

He is best known for sniffing out a German spy hiding in the bushes and pinning him down until American soldiers could get there and sort him out. Surviving a grenade explosion and other narrow escapes, he was promoted to Sergeant and was awarded many medals, even one by General Pershing (Walker, 2020).

AMAZING FACT

- *Henry Tandey was awarded the Victoria Cross in September 1918 for bravery in the Fifth Battle of Ypres and became the most decorated British private soldier in World War 1. However, he's remembered more for sparing Adolf Hitler's life in 1918, refusing to kill an unarmed soldier (Bell, 2014).*

MEDICAL

Noel Chavasse

Before joining the war, Chavasse competed in the 400-meter sprint at the 1908 Olympics ("The only VC and Bar", 2022). As part of the medical corps, he was not afraid to criticize the lack of organization he encountered on the frontlines, as well as making those in charge more aware of the reality of shell shock.

At Ypres, he won the Military Cross for rescuing soldiers for a full 15-hour shift, and a year later at the Somme, he was awarded his first Victoria Cross for saving 20 men even though he was wounded himself ("The only VC and Bar", 2022). Not done with helping those wounded in the thick of battle, he was also at Passchendaele where he went out into no-man's-land again and again even though he was suffering from a fractured skull.

On August 4, 1916, after a shell hit his first-aid post, damaging his face and causing stomach wounds, he crawled for help but died two days later ("The only VC and Bar", 2022). Again, he was awarded the VC, making him the only person to gain two in WW1.

His last words written while on his deathbed were *"Duty called and called me to obey"* ("The only VC and Bar", 2022, para. 7).

Jane Jeffrey

Born in England, Jeffrey moved to America where she trained as a nurse. When the war broke out, she volunteered to go back to Europe as part of the American Red Cross to help. Stationed east of Paris, the conditions were terrible, with no plumbing and tents as hospital wards.

On July 15, 1918, the hospital was attacked by German aircraft and bombed, killing 2 people and injuring 14, one of whom was

Jeffrey (Fausone, 2018). Why they targeted a clearly-marked medical facility is not known, but dropping bombs on nurses and doctors was not an acceptable act according to the Geneva Convention (Fausone, 2018).

The news article on the bombing read:

Miss Jane Jeffrey, the only Red Cross nurse who was wounded, was struck near the spine by a piece of metal that traversed the entire length of a ward only a few inches above a long row of mostly surgical cases and penetrated the end wall of the tent outside of which she was standing (Fausone, 2018, para. 29).

Even though she was severely injured, Jeffrey remained to help others. This act of service gained her the French Legion of Honor award and the US Distinguished Service Cross.

Edith Cavell

Cavell was in charge of a hospital in Belgium that took in victims of the war and reminded the nurses to help anyone who came in, no matter what side they were on. In August 1914, the country was taken over by the Germans, and she saw an opportunity to help British, Belgian, and French soldiers to escape to Holland.

Working with a secret network, she smuggled over 200 men from the hospital, through an underground tunnel, and out of the country ("WW1 heroes", 2020). Cavell made sure they had money, fake identity cards, and passwords to ensure they were not discovered. She even took 175 of the soldiers into her own home, hiding them until the time was right to escape.

The German police became suspicious of men disappearing and soon began to focus their attention on the hospital. Friends urged Cavell to leave Belgium, but she saw her work as too important. On August 3, 1915, she was arrested after a spy discovered the underground tunnel beneath the hospital. Many countries pleaded with Germany to release Cavell or give her a light sentence, but she was executed by firing squad on October 12th ("WW1 heroes", 2020).

After the war, a large memorial service was held for her in London, and a statue was erected near Trafalgar Square with the words "Humanity, Fortitude, Devotion, and Sacrifice" on it. She is remembered as one of the pioneers of modern nursing.

Louise Thuliez

Thuliez was a French teacher whose village was invaded. As she was helping the wounded British soldiers left behind, she became involved in the resistance. Looking for more ways in which she could help "defeat" the Germans, she got involved with Edith Cavell who she worked with. In 1915, she began secretly smuggling Allied patients across to Cavell's house.

German surveillance began to focus on the hospital and the nurses, and soon she was caught along with Cavell. She was sentenced to death as well, but because of international pressure, it was changed to life imprisonment. When the war finished, she received the Legion d'Honneur and the Croix de Guerre for her daring work.

When WW2 broke out, Thuliez was back again in her role as nurse smuggling Allied patients back to safety!

COMMUNICATIONS

Grace Banker

Telephones were a very important tool for getting messages across, and it quickly became clear that normal soldiers were not very good at this task. So, General Pershing asked for any volunteers to join the troops to man the telephones. A group of 223 women signed up and were soon called the "Hello Girls" (Timbie, 2021).

Some stayed at headquarters while a select few were stationed near the frontlines. 33 bilingual speakers worked under Grace Banker in these tough conditions, connecting critical calls between the Allied forces. She writes in her diary about what it was like to be at the battles of St. Mihiel and Meuse-Argonne:

The cannons are roaring. 12 midnight. Capt. Scott, Miss Russell and myself went outside for a minute to look at the sky. There are great flashes of light all along the horizon like Northern Lights. 2:50am, the night railroad guns are beginning to roar… such a noise. Worse than a heavy surf in a storm. The old flimsy barracks shake and the beds rock as though in a miniature earthquake… (Timbie, 2021, para. 3).

150,000 calls a day were connected by these switchboard operators, helping commanders to communicate vital information. For her role in the war, Banker received the Distinguished Service Medal.

Cher Ami

Using pigeons, dogs, and runners was still a very crucial part of sending messages in the war. 442 pigeons were sent during the Meuse-Argonne Offensive at the end of 1918 ("Cher Ami", 2020). A commander would write a brief note and give it to a Signal Corps officer who would put it in a small capsule attached to the bird's leg. The pigeon would fly back to its coop where it would trigger a bell when it landed, notifying the officer there that a message had come in.

Cher Ami (meaning "Dear Friend" in French) was a carrier pigeon that flew 12 important messages across the frontlines in 1918 ("Cher Ami", 2020). One of her most important was from Major Whittlesey when he and his unit was surrounded by enemy troops. From 500 men, they were down to only 200, and they urgently needed assistance to get out of there alive.

Whittlesey had sent out a few pigeons to tell his commanders where he was, but the messages did not get through. Often enemy soldiers would shoot at the birds, knowing they were carrying important communications. The Americans began to fire at the ravine with their artillery to provide support, accidentally bombing Whittlesey and his men.

Using Cher Ami, his last pigeon, the major sent this message: *"We are along the road parallel to 276.4. Our own artillery is dropping a barrage directly on us. For heaven's sake, stop it"* ("Cher Ami", 2020, para. 16). The Germans opened fire as they saw the bird take off, but she made it 25 miles to deliver the note and save the 200 men.

Later, she was shot during one of her missions and lost her leg. Cher Ami was personally put on a boat back to the States by General Pershing himself. The brave pigeon was awarded the French *Croix de Guerre* - Cross of War.

SPIES

Marthe Cnoclaert

Cnoclaert was training to be a doctor in Belgium when it was invaded. She was conscripted to work as a nurse in a hospital tending to soldiers, but her loyalty was always to her own country, not Germany. So, when a British spymaster asked her to help, she jumped at the chance to be part of the war.

Her first mission was to gather as much information as she could about Roulers station, an important location for the German war movements. Because of the details she provided, the Allies carried out a precision bombing of the target in the spring of 1915 ("Spies", n.d.).

Still a nurse, she was on call when the first gas attack victims came in and worked around the clock to care for them. This earned her the German Iron Cross for her dedication. They even asked if she would spy for them, but she refused!

In November 1916, she was arrested after the Germans became suspicious and laid a trap for her. After planting explosives near a German ammo dump, she left her watch behind, engraved with her initials. She was found guilty of espionage and sentenced to death, but the head doctor spoke out about her loyalty, and she was thrown in prison instead. After the war, she was presented with British, French, and Belgian honors, making her the only person to be decorated by the four main armies of World War 1 ("Spies", n.d.).

Gabrielle Petit

Furious that the Germans had invaded her country, Petit wanted to gather information and send it to the Allies to help. She was invited to London to be trained as a spy. After her time there, she went back to Belgium where she carefully put together a spy network. Traveling between France and her own country, she delivered top-secret data about the different areas the Germans were in and what they were doing.

She was caught and arrested on January 20, 1916, and thrown in jail ("Spies", n.d.). Every time the Germans interrogated her, she told them how much she hated them. At her trial, she only spoke French and was sentenced to death by firing squad.

It was only after the war that her work as a spy was recognized, and she was awarded the Croix de l'Ordre de Léopold in May 1919 ("Spies", n.d.). A statue was erected in her honor at Brussels' Place St Jean.

Mata Hari

Born in the Netherlands, Margaretha Zelle became an exotic dancer and changed her name to Mata Hari. She became very popular among wealthy and powerful men, especially high-ranking government officials. Because the Netherlands remained neutral during the war, she was able to travel freely between countries, meeting up with her different admirers.

Using her relationships, she traded gossip, picked up information, and was approached by more than one spymaster in Germany and France to help in the war effort. Whether she actually became a spy is still not confirmed, but Mata Hari's movements and behavior became very suspicious. One of her admirers was a German Major named Arnold Kalle, who decided to send a false coded message he knew the French would intercept. She was arrested in Paris in February 1917 with a closed trial five months later (Cavanaugh, 2017).

The French were looking for someone to blame for their defeats and wanted to pin the deaths of 50,000 French soldiers on this supposed spy (Cavanaugh, 2017). In July, she was dragged out before the firing squad where she refused to wear a blindfold. Mata Hari died without the truth of her involvement ever being revealed.

14

HOW THE WAR CHANGED THE WORLD

The modern world had truly been born as a result of WW1. Nations and families were still grieving after the deaths of so many soldiers. Old empires crumbled, making way for maps to be redrawn and borders to be changed. Colonial states looked to break free from their masters, and revolutions threatened political systems that had stood for centuries. Communism lifted its head for the first time as Russia underwent a massive change, and the United States began to step out as a recognized world power.

Many countries were simply trying to find their own feet in the midst of a changing world. The "war to end all wars" was a promise that never came true, and any chance for real peace was doomed once the blame for WW1 was shifted onto Germany.

There were many other changes: socially as women played a larger role in society, technology became an important part of everyday life, and economics shifted the balance of power between nations.

GEO-POLITICAL

Four empires collapsed at the end of WW1. Each of them had been looking for glory and territory, but as their armies were defeated, they could no longer continue to rule as they had for so many years. Smaller countries emerged, changing the borders of Europe into a new multi-cultural continent.

Russia

Russia was the first to undergo a change of leadership and politics. Although the transformation wasn't a result of losing the war like the Central Powers, disappointment with the tsar and his upper class fueled a revolution. Many people were not happy with the decision to go to war in the first place, and once the disastrous effects of the army's defeat began to set in, workers and peasants rose up.

Tsar Nicholas II was an unpopular ruler and his dealings with Rasputin did not help win him any support. Already suffering while the Russin aristocracy lived in luxury, the citizens of the country rose up behind promises of change from Vladimir Lenin. A dynamic young man, his ideas to break the hierarchy and give power back to the people were easily accepted. After the defeats of Tannenberg and Gorlice-Tarnow, it became clear that the war was not in the best interests of the country, and the Bolshevik Revolution occurred (Cameron, 2014).

Once Tsar Nicholas II was overthrown and killed, the way for a new order opened. Communism would play a major part in the world for the next 70 years as Russia embraced the new political system that became known through WW2 and the Cold War.

AMAZING FACT

- *It was the Germans who supplied the train with their own soldiers to transport Lenin into Russia as part of their plan to help destabilize the country so that it would pull out of the war (Widmer, 2017).*

Austria-Hungary

The Habsburg Monarchy had ruled for a long time in central Europe, but it all came to an end when the empire was dissolved. Paying for its part in the war, a treaty was forced on the nation, splitting it up. Austria and Hungary were no longer one entity and were separated. Poland was freed from the Habsburg rule, and Czechoslovakia and Yugoslavia became two independent countries (Cameron, 2014).

All territory gained in the war was lost and Austria had to pay back war reparations to compensate for the damage it had done.

Ottoman Empire

It was no surprise when the Ottomans finally gave up its rule of the Mediterranean. It had already been losing power and authority before the war, and its partnership with the Central Powers sealed the empire's fate once the war ended. In 1922, when the last Ottoman Sultan, Mehmed VI, stepped down, the once-great nation was dismantled, making way for a new modern Turkey under Mustafa Ataturk (Cameron, 2014). France and Britain drew a line down the middle of the other countries once owned by the Ottomans and took control of those. This controversial line would cause countless issues later on, especially between Israel and Palestine .

JAMES BURROWS

Germany

One of the main instigators of the whole war, Germany was heavily punished. One of the demands of the Treaty of Versailles was that they give up certain areas they had once controlled, such as Alsace-Lorraine, which they had taken from France. The Rhineland also became a demilitarized zone, occupied by Allied troops. Poland, Belgium, Denmark, and parts of Russia were returned. (Interestingly, these were some of Hitler's first targets when he began his WW2 campaign!).

The German Empire lost 13% of its territory when it was stripped of its colonies, and the Kaiser was forced to abdicate his throne (Cameron, 2014). A shaky republic was set up which left and right-wing political groups began trying to dominate. Some wanted another monarchy, while others were fighting the rise of communism. It was during this time of instability and economic depression that Adolf Hitler rose to power.

FALSE PEACE

Instead of being a war that brought an end to all the fighting, what happened after WW1 only seemed to make things worse.

The countries that had started the war needed to pay for what they had done. This was the reason for the Treaty of Versailles, a document that was drawn up dictating the conditions for the Central Powers who had been involved in causing the conflict. But instead of peace, it was more like a big stick that humiliated, embarrassed, and hurt those countries to the point of becoming angry and resentful.

Led by Great Britain, France, the US, and Italy (The Big Four), the treaty handed down harsh terms, specifically on Germany. Instead of using all of Woodrow Wilson's 14 points, which he believed would bring "peace without victory," the western powers focused on reducing armies, stripping land away, and demanding repayment for war damages ("Treaty of Versailles", 2019). France's premier, Georges Clemenceau, made sure that Germany got the harshest punishment possible in its "war guilt" clause.

Rather than paving the way for countries to rebuild in peace, the treaty caused dissatisfaction and bitterness. A large affair was held at the Palace of Versailles in France, although there were many countries represented there, the only ones with real power to make decisions were Britain, France, and America. In the end, France pushed hard for a full punishment to be dealt out, since it had suffered the worst out of the Allies. Although Italy and Japan had also contributed during the war, these were not given the respect they felt they deserved at the conference. Both countries felt they were not given certain territories they had been promised for their part in the war and felt snubbed by the more powerful nations. These were feelings that Mussolini, Hitler, and the Japanese generals used to great effect in their own political campaigns.

The League of Nations was another of Wilson's points that brought countries together to ensure peace, but it lacked any real authority when his own country refused to be a part of it. Without America to back it, there was not enough authority to deal with the issues that sprang up in the years that followed. Germany, Japan, and Italy saw it as a club of WW1 victors, and soon began to act in defiance of the league.

On top of this, a number of wars and struggles broke out across the region, some of them worse than the battles that had been fought in WW1. After the Russian Revolution, there were disputes over borders which led to fighting, and other countries looked to be independent.

These wars included the Finnish Civil War, which set up the independent state of Finland. The Estonian-Soviet War and the Latvian-Soviet War did the same for Estonia and Latvia. And

Poland fought with Russia, Ukraine, and Lithuania to solidify its own borders. Greece fought against occupying forces, while Ireland and Egypt wanted to throw off the hold Britain had on them.

It wasn't until 1923 that the region calmed down into what looked like peace, although beneath the surface there was much tension boiling up again.

SOCIAL

The war reshaped the way societies functioned. The role of the upper class no longer had the status it once did, and in certain countries like Russia, it was attacked and dismantled to make way for a larger working class under Communism. Germany saw the same happen as the old aristocracy fell once the kaiser abdicated, as did Austria and Turkey. Even in Britain, class structure was shaken as many soldiers and officers that had died had come from this social ranking (Cameron, 2014).

The rise of workers as a powerful force swept through Europe as trade unions promised lower classes greater political and social representation (Cameron, 2014). Common people began demanding their rights in more countries, sparking revolutions.

But one of the biggest changes was the role of women in society. Jobs that had always been kept for men, were suddenly filled with women as husbands, fathers, and sons marched off to war. Traditionally seen as people who should stay at home and care for children, females were now capable of working in factories. By 1918, one in every ten workers in munitions was a woman ("How did WW1", 2018). Some ladies became conductors on buses, some worked on farms, while others took on important positions in other male-dominated jobs.

Statue commemorating women during the war

Because of their work in factories, many women no longer wore dresses, and for the first time, the fashion was to not wear corsets, but trousers and short hair. The biggest advancement for women in Britain was when some of them won the right to vote in February 1918 and the Sex Disqualification (Removal) Act of 1919 which allowed them to do men's jobs ("How did WW1", 2018).

EPIDEMIC

If dealing with the 20 million deaths from WW1 was not enough, after all the fighting there was more to come. This time it was from disease. Although it was called the Spanish Flu (because it was reported in newspapers there more than anywhere else), it probably originated in other countries, and early cases were recorded in

Kansas, US in the spring of 1918 (Zelazko, 2020). The movement of troops helped to spread it quickly across Europe as soldiers were housed together for long periods. By the summer, Russia, Africa, Asia, and New Zealand all had cases.

At first, it was not so bad, more of a mild flu, but a second wave picked up and people began getting pneumonia, sometimes dying within two days (Zelazko, 2020)! Social distancing helped to bring the number of deaths down, but a third wave swept across the globe causing more fatalities.

The number of people who died from the virus is not officially known, but in India alone, it claimed 12.5 million lives, while US had around 550,000, adding to the world's total of around 50 million—more than the deaths from WW1 (Zelazko, 2020).

TECHNOLOGY

The industrial revolution brought so many new inventions and ways of doing things faster and more efficiently. The combustion engine changed transport, bringing cars, tanks, airplanes, and mechanized ships to the world. But there were other breakthroughs in communication and medicine.

New methods of photography, recording sounds, and wireless communication were not just useful in the war, but also in society ("How did WW1", 2018). No longer having to wait for letters or newspapers, radio became the new way to spread messages across the world instantaneously. Governments could speak to their people directly, wherever they were. Movies were used to great effect to boost morale and keep citizens updated on events.

Medically, doctors were able to save lives in war and back home with the new advances. Blood could be stockpiled and used to keep patients alive. Using sodium citrate to keep the blood from clotting, US army medic Captain Oswald Robertson, set up the first blood bank on the Western Front in 1917 ("How did WW1",

2018). When the war was over, this proved incredibly useful in city hospitals, saving many people. The Thomas Splint was used, reversing the four in every five soldiers who died from broken legs, to four out of five surviving from 1916 onward ("How did WW1", 2018).

Other medical advances used in the war and brought back to the cities were tuberculosis screenings, tetanus treatments, typhoid vaccines, prevention of venereal diseases, and disinfection used in surgery.

All the technological inventions and new methods were not just beneficial for war but increased the standard of living for normal citizens too. The world was becoming more and more connected and modern.

FINANCIAL

The war was an incredible financial strain on every country that took part. It cost millions to train, arm, and feed whole armies, as well as build new weapons. By 1918, a day's worth of bullets alone cost £3.8 million ($4.5 million) ("How did WW1", 2018). It's no surprise then that Britain and others took out loans to fund their fighting. The problem came after the war when they had to begin paying those back. With shortages of food and other resources, the added financial burden was heavy.

France's workforce suffered as over one million disabled soldiers returned, no longer able to work. Much of their farmland was wrecked in the war, and many bridges, roads, and other infrastructure were ruined.

It was especially harsh on countries like Germany, which was forced by the Treaty of Versailles to pay £6,600 million (£284 billion in 2021) in compensation for the damages they caused in the war ("How did WW1", 2018). By 1923, their currency was almost worthless and they had no more money to pay back the debts they owed and defaulted on (missed payments). This almost crippled them and was one of the main reasons Hitler decided to defy the western powers.

Struggling to find their feet, most nations had to grapple with the double blow of the Great Depression in 1920 and the financial crash of 1929. This instability in Europe caused much friction and pressure between countries which led to bitterness and anger.

The only one to come out on top was the United States. Mainly because it had only come into the war much later, and because its economy was not hit as hard as those in Europe, it rose up to become the leading financial power and the world's banker (Cameron, 2014).

AMAZING FACT

- *It took almost 100 years for the UK to finish paying their £7 billion ($8.4 billion) debt for World War 1, making its last installment in 2015 (Cosgrave, 2015).*
- *In 2010, Germany paid back all its loans used to make reparations.*

MEMORIALS

Somme France memorial

Remembering those who died fighting for their country and stood up for what they believed became an annual event around the world. Armistice Day, recognized as the end of the war on November 11th, was first commemorated in Britain in 1919 with two minutes' silence at 11 a.m. (Michael, 2018). Soon other commonwealth countries copied the ritual, and it became a significant calendar date.

Days to remember the fallen had been around for wars fought before, but never on such a global scale. Red poppies were used as a symbol because the red flower still bloomed after the intense fighting in west Belgium (Flanders) had completely demolished buildings, trees, and fields, churning the seeds up in the mud (Michael, 2018). After WW2, Armistice Day changed to Remembrance Day to incorporate those who had given their lives in that war as well.

Other countries have similar days with the United States observing November 11th as Veterans Day, while Russia chooses to focus on the positive involvement in WW2 by celebrating May 9th rather than the defeat of WW1. For Germany, however, remembering either war and the nation's soldiers has not been easy considering they were on the wrong side of history in both. For them, a national day of mourning is held, although much more low-key than Remembrance Day or Veterans Day.

In Britain and France after the war, there was an urgency to build large statues and plaques across the nation and at battle sites to observe those who died. This resulted in some rather epic memorials across Europe that still stand to this day.

Tyne Cot war graves near Passchendaele

The Cenotaph is the UK's national monument on Whitehall that was built in 1920 as a tribute to all those whose family and friends died in World War 1 ("Remembering the fallen", n.d.). It means "empty tomb" in Greek. Most of the dead were buried close to where they fell, so the Cenotaph symbolizes their absence and is a focal point for public mourning. The Royal Artillery Memorial and the Machine Gun Corps Memorial can both be found at Hyde Park, while the Field Marshal Earl Haig Memorial and Edith Cavell Memorial can be found in other parts of London.

France has its share of memorials but one of these involves six villages that have never been rebuilt. Destroyed during the Meuse-Argonne Offensive, they were left as a reminder of the devastation of the war ("Did you know?", 2019). Each has a mayor to look after the maintenance and the identification and proper burial of the remains of any soldiers found there.

Britain, France, and America all have tombs dedicated to an unknown soldier. Westminster Abbey (London), the Arc de Triomphe (Paris), and Arlington National Cemetry (Virginia) are all places where large crowds gather each year on November 11th to remember those who fought and died.

AMAZING FACT

- *The Menin Gate near Ypres is one of the only monuments that takes names off. With over 55,000 names of those who have no known grave, one is only removed when the remains of a soldier is found and identified ("Ypres (Menin Gate)", 2022).*
- *"Thankful villages" are the 53 villages in Britain out of 16,000 which lost no men in WW1, because all those that served came home. Unlike most other villages, these don't have war memorials to commemorate the dead.*

CONCLUSIONS

"Those that fail to learn from history, are doomed to repeat it"
–Winston Churchill

Hindsight is looking back and seeing what should have been done and what could have been done better. That's why the saying is, "It's always easier in hindsight."

It's not difficult when we already have all the facts to criticize the stupidity of losing 20 million lives over one archduke. It's easy to point fingers at General Haig and others who persisted in sending thousands of men to be slaughtered in inconclusive battles of attrition. Now, we can clearly see all the mistakes and bad decisions, but at the time, they probably seemed like good strategies that had worked before.

In the end, WW1 was a confusing, muddy grind of soldiers. Despite political motives and strategies, it all became messy so quickly. What should have taken a few months to sort out, sank into years of a deadly quagmire—a stalemate of death. And if that wasn't enough, everything was changing as it went along with new technology, ideas, and politics. Old ways had to make way for a

CONCLUSIONS

new age, and it was forced on the world in war. The modern era had a bloody childbirth on the Western Front.

Many generals in WW1 made some colossally poor choices in the beginning, resulting in unnecessary waste of human life. But it is also true that there was a definite learning curve that took place, and few of those outdated tactics were still being used by 1918. Understanding how to combine technology and soldiers into warfare began to pay off in the end. So, even they benefited from hindsight, learning from their previous failures.

History is all about seeing the errors that others have made and doing our best not to make them again. It's why WW1 was supposed to be the one war that would bring an end to the fighting once and for all. Everyone saw what went wrong the first time and did not want to make those same mistakes again. But there's another saying: "history repeats itself."

Instead of promising peace, the Treaty of Versailles was filled with many of the same issues that had caused the war in the first place. Rather than sorting out the problems, it sowed seeds of division, mistrust, and inequality between nations. Those are not feelings that will bring peace and harmony between countries. So, instead of stopping all the conflict, it created another one, even worse than the war before—WW2.

Maybe the British Prime minister, David Lloyd George, was more correct about seeing the future than Wilson when in 1916 he said, *"This war, like the next war, is a war to end war"* (Browne, 2019, para. 11). There will never be an end to fighting if we don't learn from the past. Wars will carry on unless we choose another way.

As you read this book, you are learning from history, not just about what happened, but how to help avoid others from repeating those same mistakes. Reading about WW1, we can see there must be another way, a better way if we don't want to end up in another global conflict. The past can show us how to begin working for a better future, to avoid people marching off to die unnecessarily. It's time to take off your helmet, jump out of the trenches, and appreciate each other for who we are and what we all bring to the world.

Thank you for taking this trip through the Western and Eastern Fronts with me. I am so glad you survived! The journey through history is always one that makes us better human beings in the end. If you enjoyed this ride through WW1 with me, there's always another journey.

Look out for more military history books, and sign up to my email list for more updates at james-burrows.com

ABOUT THE AUTHOR

James is an armchair military expert, developing an early interest in military history from stories told by his Grandfathers and even his Great-Grandfather, who fought at the Somme.

Whether writing about WW2 or the American Revolutionary War, James hopes to spark a healthy curiosity and love for history in today's young people.

When not working or spending time with his wife and children, James can be found walking his two beautiful black Labradors in the local countryside, pondering ideas for his next book.

REFERENCES

admin. (2022, May 17). *43 facts about the Battle of Verdun you need to know.* HistoryForce. https://historyforce.com/43-facts-about-the-battle-of-verdun-you-need-to-know

Alexander, C. (2010, September). *The shock of war.* Smithsonian. https://www.smithsonianmag.com/history/the-shock-of-war-55376701/

Alvin York: Veteran's story. (2023). Military.com. https://www.military.com/history/alvin-york-world-war-i.html

Andreajn. (2019, November 15). *101 mind-blowing WW1 facts you must know.* Facts.net. https://facts.net/ww1-facts/

Andrews, E. (2019, January 15). *10 things you may not know about the Battle of Verdun.* HISTORY. https://www.history.com/news/10-things-you-may-not-know-about-the-battle-of-verdun

Badsey, S. (2016). *Amiens, Battle of.* 1914-1918-Online.net. https://encyclopedia.1914-1918-online.net/article/amiens_battle_of

Baker, C. (2019). *Life in the trenches of the First World War.* Longlongtrail.co.uk. https://www.longlongtrail.co.uk/soldiers/a-soldiers-life-1914-1918/life-in-the-trenches-of-the-first-world-war/

Balfour, M. G. (2019). *William II: Emperor of Germany.* Encyclopædia Britannica. https://www.britannica.com/biography/William-II-emperor-of-Germany

Battle of Kolubara (1914). (2020, November 13). Serbia, Land of Heroes. https://serbialandofheroes.wordpress.com/english-section/battle-of-kolubara-1914/

Battle of Megiddo. (2019). National Army Museum. https://www.nam.ac.uk/explore/battle-megiddo

Battle of the Somme. (2019). National Army Museum. https://www.nam.ac.uk/explore/battle-somme

Beck, E. (2017a, April 7). *Ottoman Empire in World War I.* History Crunch. https://www.historycrunch.com/ottoman-empire-in-world-war-i.html#/

Beck, E. (2017b, September 3). *Battle of Tannenberg in World War I.* History Crunch. https://www.historycrunch.com/battle-of-tannenberg-in-world-war-i.html#/

Beck, E. (2021, September 3). *Allied Powers of World War I.* History Crunch. https://www.historycrunch.com/allied-powers-of-world-war-i.html#/

Bell, B. (2014, August 4). *World War One: The British hero who did not shoot Hitler.* BBC News. https://www.bbc.com/news/uk-england-28593256

REFERENCES

Bishop, P. (n.d.). *World War One in Numbers*. Kingston upon Hull War Memorial 1914 - 1918. https://ww1hull.com/world-war-one-in-numbers/

Blake, R., & Blake, B. (2019). *David Lloyd George: Prime minister of United Kingdom*. Encyclopædia Britannica. https://www.britannica.com/biography/David-Lloyd-George

Bronner, M. (2023). *Germany's sixteen greatest World War I heroes*. Archivaria.com. http://www.archivaria.com/WorldWarOneHeroes/SixteenGermanWarHeroes.html

Browne, A. (2019, March 3). *The Great War in words: 20 quotes by contemporaries of World War One*. History Hit. https://www.historyhit.com/the-great-war-in-words-quotes-by-contemporaries-of-world-war-one/

Budnik, R. (2019, March 12). *Lions led by donkeys: British soldiers of WW1*. War History Online https://www.warhistoryonline.com/instant-articles/lions-led-by-donkeys-soldiers.html?chrome=1&Exc_D_LessThanPoint002_p1=1

Cadman-Rivers, I. (2014, August 11). *Food during the First World War*. WW1 East Sussex. http://www.eastsussexww1.org.uk/food-first-world-war/index.html

Cameron, F. (2014, July 8). *The impact of the First World War and its implications for Europe today*. Heinrich-Böll-Stiftung. https://www.boell.de/en/2014/07/08/impact-first-world-war-and-its-implications-europe-today#:~:text=The%20-First%20World%20War%20destroyed

Cavanaugh, R. (2017, October 13). *Mata Hari's true story remains a mystery 100 years after her death*. Time. https://time.com/4977634/mata-hari-true-history/

Çetinsaya, G. (2017). *Kut al-Amara*. 1914-1918-Online.net. https://encyclopedia.1914-1918-online.net/article/kut_al-amara

Cher Ami. (2020, July 28). Home of Heroes. https://homeofheroes.com/heroes-stories/world-war-i/cher-ami/

Choi, J. (2017, April 4). *"Never think that war... is not a crime," and more defining WW1 quotes*. USA TODAY https://www.usatoday.com/story/news/world/2017/04/04/world-war-i-quotes/100031552/

Cook, T. (2015). *The Battle of Vimy Ridge*. Canadian War Museum. https://www.warmuseum.ca/the-battle-of-vimy-ridge/

Cornish, P. (2015). *Machine gun*. 1914-1918-Online.net. https://encyclopedia.1914-1918-online.net/article/machine_gun

Cornish, P. (2016). *Flamethrower*. 1914-1918-Online.net. https://encyclopedia.1914-1918-online.net/article/flamethrower

Cosgrave, J. (2015, March 9). *UK finally finishes paying for World War I*. CNBC. https://www.cnbc.com/2015/03/09/uk-finally-finishes-paying-for-world-war-i.html

REFERENCES

Cox, A. (2020, January 8). *Discover the real runners of the First World War and their incredible stories.* Findmypast https://www.findmypast.co.uk/blog/discoveries/first-world-war-runners#:~:text=What%20were%20runners%20in%20the

Crutchley, P. (2015, January 6). *Adrian Carton de Wiart: The unkillable soldier.* BBC News. https://www.bbc.com/news/magazine-30685433

Did you know? There are six towns in France that have mayors, but no residents. (2019, January 18). The Local. https://www.thelocal.fr/20190118/did-you-know-there-are-six-towns-in-france-that-have-mayors-but-no-residents/

Douglas Haig: The chief. (2000). National Army Museum. https://www.nam.ac.uk/explore/douglas-haig

Duffy, M. (2009a). *Primary Documents - Sir Douglas Haig's "Backs to the Wall" Order, 11 April 1918.* Firstworldwar.com. https://www.firstworldwar.com/source/backstothewall.htm

Duffy, M. (2009b). *The First Battle of the Marne, 1914.* Firstworldwar.com. https://www.firstworldwar.com/battles/marne1.htm

Duffy, M. (2009c). *Who's Who - Enver Pasha.* Firstworldwar.com. https://www.firstworldwar.com/bio/enver.htm

Faith, T. I. (2016). *Gas warfare.* 1914-1918-Online.net. https://encyclopedia.1914-1918-online.net/article/gas_warfare

Fausone, J. G. (2018). *Jane Jeffrey.* Home of Heroes. https://homeofheroes.com/heroes-stories/world-war-i/jane-jeffrey/

First trenches are dug on the Western Front. (2009). History.com. https://www.history.com/this-day-in-history/first-trenches-are-dug-on-the-western-front#:~:text=In%20total%20the%20trenches%20built

Flora Sandes – A great unsung military heroine. (n.d.). The Royal Mint. https://www.royalmint.com/discover/uk-coins/first-world-war/personal-stories/flora-sandes--a-great-unsung-military-heroine/

Fowler, W. (n.d.). *A British soldier's kit in the First World War.* The History Press. https://www.thehistorypress.co.uk/articles/a-british-soldier-s-kit-in-the-first-world-war/

Furbank, K. (2018, November 9). *The story of an Irish soldier who was the youngest Allied troop to die in WW1.* Irish Mirror. https://www.irishmirror.ie/news/irish-news/story-john-condon-waterford-born-13565218

Goodridge, E. (2018, April 26). *Overlooked no more: Maria Bochkareva, who led women into battle in WW1.* The New York Times. https://www.nytimes.com/2018/04/25/obituaries/overlooked-maria-bochkareva.html

Gorlitz, W. (2019). *Erich Ludendorff:German general.* Encyclopædia Britannica. https://www.britannica.com/biography/Erich-Ludendorff

REFERENCES

Graves, R. (1957). *Good Bye To All That*. Internet Archive. https://archive.org/stream/in.ernet.dli.2015.186550/2015.186550.Good-Bye-To-All-That_djvu.txt

Guzvica, S. (2022, June 9). *Gavrilo Princip: How taking a wrong turn started World War I*. The Collector. https://www.thecollector.com/gavrilo-princip-ww1/

Harper, K. C. (2021, May 31). *Lieutenant Edouard V. Izac, the last surviving Medal of Honor recipient from WW1*. Congressional Medal of Honor Society. https://www.cmohs.org/news-events/medal-of-honor-recipient-profile/lieutenant-edouard-v-izac-the-last-surviving-medal-of-honor-recipient-from-wwi/

Hemmings, J. (2019, January 3). *Teenage hero of the Battle of Jutland & recipient of the Victoria Cross*. War History Online.

https://www.warhistoryonline.com/world-war-i/boy-first-class-john-jack-cornwell.html?chrome=1

Hickman, K. (2017). *Beloved ace: Georges Guynemer*. ThoughtCo. https://www.thoughtco.com/georges-guynemer-2360554

Hickman, K. (2018a). *World War I: Battle of Verdun*. ThoughtCo. https://www.thoughtco.com/world-war-i-battle-of-verdun-2361415

Hickman, K. (2018b). *World War I: The Battle of Gallipoli*. ThoughtCo. https://www.thoughtco.com/world-war-i-battle-of-gallipoli-2361403

Hickman, K. (2019a). *World War I: Battle of Loos*. ThoughtCo. https://www.thoughtco.com/world-war-i-battle-of-loos-2361395

Hickman, K. (2019b). *World War I: Second Battle of Ypres*. ThoughtCo. https://www.thoughtco.com/second-battle-of-ypres-2361411

Higgins, H. (n.d.). *British Expeditionary Force (WW1) | PDF*. Scribd. Retrieved February 26, 2023, from

https://www.scribd.com/document/235917765/British-Expeditionary-Force-WW1#

How did WW1 change the world? (2018, November 9). BBC. https://www.bbc.co.uk/newsround/45966335

How President Woodrow Wilson tried to end all wars once and for all. (2018, December 28). Big Think. https://bigthink.com/the-present/president-woodrow-wilsons-vision-for-the-league-of-nations-still-inspires/

John J. Pershing. (2018, August 21). History.com. https://www.history.com/topics/world-war-i/john-j-pershing

Johnson, B. (2017). *World War 1 Timeline - 1914*. Historic UK. https://www.historic-uk.com/HistoryUK/HistoryofBritain/World-War-1-Timeline-1914/

Jorgensen, T. (2017, October 11). *How Marie Curie brought x-ray machines to the battlefield*. Smithsonian Magazine. https://www.smithsonianmag.com/history/how-marie-curie-brought-x-ray-machines-to-battlefield-180965240/#:~:text=During%20World%20War%20I%2C%20the

REFERENCES

Joseph Joffre. (n.d.). Heritage History. https://www.heritage-history.com/index.php?c=resources&s=char-dir&f=joffre

Keep, J. L. H. (2019). *Nicholas II Biography, death, & facts*. Encyclopædia Britannica. https://www.britannica.com/biography/Nicholas-II-tsar-of-Russia#ref5260

Kennedy, M. D. (2016). *Tanks and Tank Warfare*. 1914-1918-Online.net. https://encyclopedia.1914-1918-online.net/article/tanks_and_tank_warfare

Kiilleen, A. (2017, November 8). *Japan's victory in World War I*. U.S. Naval Institute. https://www.usni.org/magazines/naval-history-magazine/2021/june/japans-victory-world-war-i

Lang, Dr. S. (2014, September). *10 facts you (probably) didn't know about the First World War*. HistoryExtra. https://www.historyextra.com/period/first-world-war/facts-first-world-war-one-ww1-armistice-dates-triple-alliance-triple-entente/

Lascurettes, K. (2017). *The Concert of Europe and great-power governance today: What can the order of 19th-century Europe teach policymakers about international order in the 21st century?* RAND Corporation. https://doi.org/10.7249/pe226

Lehnardt, K. (2016). *75 interesting facts about World War I*. Factretriever.com. https://www.factretriever.com/world-war-i-facts

Lein, R. (2018). *Offensive, Gorlice-Tarnow*. 1914-1918-Online.net. https://encyclopedia.1914-1918-online.net/article/offensive_gorlice-tarnow

Lesser known facts about The Battle of the Somme. (2023). HISTORY Channel. https://www.history.co.uk/articles/lesser-known-facts-about-the-battle-of-the-somme

Life in the trenches. (2000). NZ History. https://nzhistory.govt.nz/war/new-zealanders-in-belgium/a-soldiers-lot

Limbach, R. (2016). *Schlieffen Plan: German military history*. Encyclopædia Britannica. https://www.britannica.com/event/Schlieffen-Plan

McEvoy, W. (2009). *Battles - The First Battle of Ypres, 1914*. firstworldwar.com. https://www.firstworldwar.com/battles/ypres1.htm

McRae, J. (1915). *In Flanders fields*. Poetry Foundation. https://www.poetryfoundation.org/poems/47380/in-flanders-fields

Michael, S. (2018, November 15). *Effects of World War 1*. History on the Net. https://www.historyonthenet.com/effects-of-world-war-1

Monnerville, G. (1998). *Georges Clemenceau - Leadership during World War I*. Encyclopedia Britannica. https://www.britannica.com/biography/Georges-Clemenceau/Leadership-during-World-War-I

Norwich University Online. *Six causes of World War I*. (2017, August 1). https://online.norwich.edu/academic-programs/resources/six-causes-of-world-war-i

1915: Early trench battles. (n.d.). National Army Museum. https://www.nam.ac.uk/explore/1915-early-trench-battles

REFERENCES

Owen, W. (1920). *Dulce Et Decorum Est*. Poetry Foundation. https://www.poetry foundation.org/poems/46560/dulce-et-decorum-est

Philpott, W. (2014). *Somme, Battles of. 1914-1918-Online.net*. https://encyclopedia.1914-1918-online.net/article/somme_battles_of

Potts, L., & Rimmer, M. (2017, May 20). *The Canary Girls: The workers the war turned yellow*. BBC News. https://www.bbc.com/news/uk-england-39434504

Rees, S. (2009). *The Christmas Truce*. Firstworldwar.com. https://www.firstworldwar.com/features/christmastruce.htm

Remembering the fallen: Six London WW1 memorials. (n.d.). English Heritage. https://www.english-heritage.org.uk/visit/london-statues-and-monuments/london-WW1-memorials/

Rickard, J. (2001, March 14). *Siege of Liege, 5-16 August 1914 (Belgium)*. historyofwar.org. http://www.historyofwar.org/articles/battles_liege.html

Roller, S. (2021, November 9). *10 facts about Lord Kitchener*. History Hit. https://www.historyhit.com/facts-about-lord-kitchener/

Routledge, P. (2021, September 8). *Deadliest explosion killed 10,000 Germans and was heard 140 miles away in London*. Mirror. https://www.mirror.co.uk/news/uk-news/deadliest-explosion-killed-10000-germans-24939714

Roy, R. H., & Foot, R. (2023, February 22). *Battle of Passchendaele*. Encyclopedia Britannica. https://www.britannica.com/event/Battle-of-Passchendaele#ref334326

Russia attacks - Brusilov offensive. (n.d.). Royal Irish. https://www.royal-irish.com/events/russia-attacks-brusilov-offensive

Royde-Smith, J. G., & Showalter, D. E. (2018). *World War I : Facts, Causes, & History*. Encyclopedia Britannica. https://www.britannica.com/event/World-War-I

Seaver, C. (2022, November 1). *How did the "Balkan Powder Keg" lead to WW1?* History Defined. https://www.historydefined.net/balkan-powder-keg/

Sheffield, G. (2011, March 10). *The Western Front: Lions led by donkeys?* BBC. https://www.bbc.co.uk/history/worldwars/wwone/lions_donkeys_01.shtml

Spies. (n.d.). Never Such Innocence. https://www.neversuchinnocence.com/spies-first-world-war

Stewart, R. (2005). *American Military History Vol. II: The United States Army in a Global Era, 1917-2003*. Dept. of the Army.

Swift, J. (2019). *Brusilov Offensive*. Encyclopædia Britannica. https://www.britannica.com/event/Brusilov-Offensive-1916

Victoria Cross (VC). (n.d.). The Gazette. https://www.thegazette.co.uk/awards-and-accreditation/content/100077

Tactics in warfare during World War I. (2022). DVA. https://anzacportal.dva.gov.au/wars-and-missions/ww1/military-organisation/tactics-in-warfare

The lessons of history famous quotations and quotes lessons from history. (n.d.). Age-of-The-

Sage.org. https://www.age-of-the-sage.org/history/quotations/lessons_of_history.html

The 10 bloodiest battles of WWI. (2023). NZ Herald. https://www.nzherald.co.nz/world/the-10-bloodiest-battles-of-wwi/UVT7THOUP2WQPNQDOB5UIC5XDM/

The War Cross 1914-1918 - French medals & awards, WW1. (2018, December 5). Identify Medals. https://www.identifymedals.com/database/medals-by-period/ww1-medals/the-war-cross-1914-1918/

Tikkanen, A. (2019). *Albert I: king of Belgium.* Encyclopædia Britannica. https://www.britannica.com/biography/Albert-I-king-of-Belgium

Timbie, C. (2021). *100 years ago "Hello Girl" Grace Banker receives Distinguished Service Medal.* worldwar1centennial.org. https://www.worldwar1centennial.org/index.php/communicate/press-media/WW1-centennial-news/6250-100-years-ago-hello-girl-grace-banker-receives-distinguished-service-medal.html

The Kaiser, the Tsar and King George V - cousins at war in WW1. (n.d.). HISTORY Channel. https://www.history.co.uk/articles/the-kaiser-the-tsar-and-king-george-v-cousins-at-war-in-ww1

The only VC and Bar of WW1. (2022). Royal British Legion. https://www.britishlegion.org.uk/stories/the-only-vc-and-bar-of-the-first-world-war

32 interesting facts about World War I. (2020, August 31). History Colored. https://historycolored.com/articles/5310/32-interesting-facts-about-world-war-i

Treaty of Versailles. (2019). USHMM. https://encyclopedia.ushmm.org/content/en/article/treaty-of-versailles

Tworek, H. (2014). *Wireless telegraphy.* 1914-1918-Online.net. https://encyclopedia.1914-1918-online.net/article/wireless_telegraphy

Walker, S. (2020, June 28). *Sergeant Stubby, the most decorated war dog of WW1, c. 1920.* HistoryColored. https://historycolored.com/photos/5054/sergeant-stubby-the-most-decorated-war-dog-of-ww1-c-1920/

Watson, A. (2016). *German Spring Offensives 1918.* 1914-1918-Online.net. https://encyclopedia.1914-1918-online.net/article/german_spring_offensives_1918

Wernitz, F. (2014, October 8). *Iron Cross.* 1914-1918-Online.net. https://encyclopedia.1914-1918-online.net/article/iron_cross

Why whales were vital in the First World War. (2023). IWM. https://www.iwm.org.uk/history/why-whales-were-vital-in-the-first-world-war#:~:text=Inside%20the%20trenches%2C%20British%20soldiers

Widmer, T. (2017, April 20). *Lenin and the Russian Spark.* The New Yorker. https://www.newyorker.com/culture/culture-desk/lenin-and-the-russian-spark

REFERENCES

World War I battles: Timeline. (2021, April 8). History.com. https://www.history.com/topics/world-war-i/world-war-i-battles-timeline

World War I: First Battle of the Marne. (2023). Ducksters. https://www.ducksters.com/history/world_war_i/first_battle_of_the_marne.php#:~:text=Interesting%20Facts%20about%20the%20First%20Battle%20of%20the%20-Marne&text=This%20was%20the%20first%20major

WW1 heroes everyone should know. (2020, November 6). Imagining History. https://www.imagininghistory.co.uk/post/WW1-heroes

World War I Medal of Honor recipients. (2022). PMML. https://www.pritzkermilitary.org/explore/museum/past-exhibits/lest-we-forget-doughboys-sammies-and-sailors-great-war/world-war-i-medal-honor-recipients#:~:text=126%20Medals%20of%20Honor%20were

Zabecki, D. (2015). *Military developments of World War I.* 1914-1918-Online.net. https://encyclopedia.1914-1918-online.net/article/military_developments_of_world_war_i

Zelazko, A. (2020, September 28). *How long did the flu pandemic of 1918 last?* Encyclopedia Britannica. https://www.britannica.com/story/how-long-did-the-flu-pandemic-of-1918-last

Ypres (Menin Gate): The Living Memorial to the Missing. (2022, November 3). CWGC. https://www.cwgc.org/our-work/blog/ypres-menin-gate-a-living-memorial-to-the-missing/

IMAGE REFERENCES

2204574. (2016, April 28). *Philippe Petain* [Image]. Pixabay. https://pixabay.com/photos/philately-stamps-collection-1349002/

903115. (2017, March 30). *WW1 trench warfare* [Image]. Pixabay. https://pixabay.com/photos/ww1-trench-warfare-one-war-world-2187095/

Austrian National Library. (2019, December 11). *Barracks built into the ground* [Image]. Unsplash. https://unsplash.com/photos/0_JuDagm1Ug

British Library. (2019, November 18). *Church in Laventie, France, wrecked by German bombs* [Image]. https://unsplash.com/photos/OyTa8LZxFU0

British Library. (2019, November 18). *Highland Territorials in a trench* [Image]. Unsplash. https://unsplash.com/photos/GQ5ELi84owE

British Library. (2019, November 18). *Signals office* [Image]. Unsplash. https://unsplash.com/photos/Km6TyVXFFmU

British Library. (2019, November 18). *Tommies eating in a trench* [Image]. Unsplash. https://unsplash.com/photos/i3sU1kP55fc

British Library. (2019, November 18). *X-ray room at Kitchener Hospital* [Image]. Unsplash. https://unsplash.com/photos/lOEC0VUCp2c

REFERENCES

British Library. (2019, November 26). *Sopwith Camel plane* [Image]. Unsplash. https://unsplash.com/photos/GezFpjXHoiw

Gary Butterfield. (2019, June 22). *Women steel statue* [Image]. Unsplash. https://unsplash.com/photos/KsFlb3Q5zwg

KovalevSergei. (2021, March 5). *Mark Tank* [Image]. Pixabay. https://pixabay.com/photos/mark-weapons-armored-car-cars-lnr-6070831/

Libraryofscotland. (2023, February 14). *Helmet saves head from shrapnel* [Image]. Unsplash. https://unsplash.com/photos/pUmEYj08tP0

Museums Victoria. (2019, October 23). *Anzac Day parade in London, 1919* [Image]. https://unsplash.com/photos/Xraf7hjBGSc

Museums Victoria. (2019, October 23). *Town of Lille completely destroyed* [Image]. https://unsplash.com/photos/CzsHs8A87Y0

Museums Victoria. (2019, November 11). *Coastal guns in Middle East, 1918* [Image]. Unsplash. https://unsplash.com/photos/udKsjyYNDnQ

Nypl. (2020, January 24). *Tanks moving along road* [Image]. Unsplash. https://unsplash.com/photos/pk5Bcsm3UZ8

SJTUK. (2022, May 7). *Somme France memorial* [Image]. Pixabay. https://pixabay.com/photos/somme-france-memorial-7223495/

Unseen Histories. (2021, November 8). *Wall Street celebrates on the day Germany surrendered* [Image]. Unsplash. https://unsplash.com/photos/ZHwwQDZeFVY

WikiImages. (2012, December 21). *Hindenburg, Kaiser Wilhelm, Ludendorff* [Image]. Pixabay. https://pixabay.com/photos/kaiser-wilhelm-ii-63116/

WikiImages. (2013, January 3). *Machine gun soldiers front troops* [Image]. Pixabay. https://pixabay.com/photos/machine-gun-soldiers-front-troops-67470/

Printed in Great Britain
by Amazon